To Barbara

Open your eyes to see
                    God's miracles

Open your ears to hear
                    God's miracles

Open your heart to receive
                    God's miracles

                    Theresa
                    Orecchia

ALSO BY TM ORECCHIA

Hear Their Voices

Receive Their Messages

Whispering Messages

SEE THEIR MIRACLES

Enlightened Series

T M ORECCHIA

BALBOA.
PRESS

A DIVISION OF HAY HOUSE

Balboa Press books may be ordered through booksellers or by contacting:

Balboa Press
A Division of Hay House
1663 Liberty Drive
Bloomington, IN 47403
www.balboapress.com
1 (877) 407-4847

Because of the dynamic nature of the Internet, any web addresses or links contained in this book may have changed since publication and may no longer be valid. The views expressed in this work are solely those of the author and do not necessarily reflect the views of the publisher, and the publisher hereby disclaims any responsibility for them.

The author of this book does not dispense medical advice or prescribe the use of any technique as a form of treatment for physical, emotional, or medical problems without the advice of a physician, either directly or indirectly. The intent of the author is only to offer information of a general nature to help you in your quest for emotional and spiritual well-being. In the event you use any of the information in this book for yourself, which is your constitutional right, the author and the publisher assume no responsibility for your actions.

Any people depicted in stock imagery provided by Getty Images are models, and such images are being used for illustrative purposes only.
Certain stock imagery © Getty Images.

Print information available on the last page.

ISBN: 978-1-9822-0916-2 (sc)
ISBN: 978-1-9822-0914-8 (hc)
ISBN: 978-1-9822-0915-5 (e)

Library of Congress Control Number: 2018908738

Balboa Press rev. date: 08/01/2018

CONTENTS

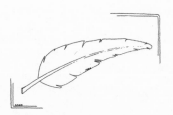

ACKNOWLEDGEMENTS

I would like to thank all the angels in this book who came to give enlightenment to the true meaning of miracles. They explained very clearly how miracles impact people in different ways and in every walk of life. Their stories cover subjects where I had never thought of looking for miracles to occur. Thank you, angels, for showing me the kindness of God who wants all humans to succeed while they are on earth.

My books would not be complete without the untiring help from my husband, Michael. This is my fourth book that he has expertly helped me edit. I truly appreciate his love, support and time for my projects. Thank you, Michael, from the bottom of my heart. Our life together has been full of many miracles, big and small.

A special thank you to my niece, Peyton, who is the angel in the mountains that completes this book.

And many, many thanks to my nephew, Ron F. Sill, for his expert artwork, designs, and advice for all of my books. A special thumbs-up for his extensive research into the unique illustrations representing the archangels' names associated with each story. Thank you, Ron, it is always a pleasure to work with you.

-Theresa

DEDICATION

Miracles from God occur many times each day. They occur all over the world and they impact people in all walks of life. Writing about the many miracles that occur on earth has opened my eyes to the power and presence of angels in everyone's life. Many people would not be alive today if not for the persistent work of angels and archangels. They are powerful entities of God and I believe they should be acknowledged. Our life takes on a whole new meaning when we allow them to walk with us.

No matter the circumstance, be it illness, injury, loss, or loneliness, God's angels willingly and happily guide each and every human being on their individual path of healing. I know…I was there. The time it takes to heal depends on you because the angels never leave you in your time of need. If you fight them, if you don't acknowledge they are with you, if you don't invite them into your life, they are unable to help you because your heart is not open to receive their healing messages.

I happily dedicate this book of 'miracles' to all the angels who came to me with their words of wisdom, teaching, and love. The world is truly a magnificent place with the power and presence of angels.

-Theresa

INTRODUCTION

I never thought too much about miracles, what they are or their true meaning. I always just listened in awe when I read or heard about the details of a near-death experience. As I grew spiritually, I would think about WHY a person returned to earth following a horrific accident. I always liked to hear the descriptions of heaven and the voices telling a soul that it was not their time to transition from earth to heaven. I paid particular attention to the messages that urged that soul to return to earth. Near-death miracles were the only miracles I acknowledged until I started writing this book on miracles.

As the angels described the true essence of a miracle, I looked around and started to see miracles happening in all walks of life. Some were more notable than others and received publicity in the news. I found Facebook to be another source to describe the occurrences of miracles.

I learned from the angels that miracles include not only miraculous cures for the body but also miraculous cures for the spirit. The angels also taught me that miracles are intended not only for one particular person but also for those who witnessed the event, for those who had an active part in the event and also for those who received the information via friends, relatives, and social media.

This information put a new meaning on the word 'miracle' to me. I began to listen more intently to the changing events in the world. I looked at them differently. I looked for the REASON a significant change occurred in a person ridden with cancer, or a homeless person walking away from a drifting life to become an asset to society, or a life-long drug addict who reached out for help and returned to help his fellow addicts. My eyes were opened to miracles that were happening not only around me but also around the world.

As with my earlier books, angels are narrating the stories. They explain very clearly, at the beginning of each story, the type of miracle they want to talk about. They further explain what the miracle is when it occurs, how they work with souls individually, all the souls who are involved in the miracle and how the miracle applies to you. To help you more clearly understand their messages about miracles, the angels dictated their information in story form.

Please enjoy this 'walk of miracles' with the angels. Look around after each story and see the miracles that surround you daily.

-*Theresa*

You will receive a miracle in one hour if you type 'Amen' and share this photo.

She truly is a miracle child to have survived the accident.

I think that I am seeing a miracle…that man just survived a fire that gutted his house.

The only survivor of the horrible plane crash was a little baby… now THAT is a miracle.

Do these good deeds and say this prayer for one week and you will receive a miracle.

EXACTLY WHAT IS A MIRACLE?

On the human side, a miracle is perceived as an instantaneous and significant change in a person's life that is incomprehensible as to how it was able to occur.

On the spiritual side, there are many angels watching and interceding on earth to protect and even rescue souls from impending danger and destruction. Angels are also working to direct souls to sources that are able to help them recover their broken or sickened lives on earth and direct them to God.

Many people use the word 'miracle' loosely believing that ANYTHING good that happens to them is a miracle. Now, the changing of a red light to a green light when you are driving is NOT a miracle on the spiritual side.

Many 'pray' for a miracle. So, exactly what are they praying for? Is it for a physical healing? Is it for financial success? Is it for a loved one to not die? Is it for peace in the family or the world?

When you are told that a miracle will come your way within a certain amount of time after you perform a specific task, what are you expecting…a windfall of money, a new car, or even a new house?

We angels would like to take you on a journey to show you the human and spiritual side of the many miracles that are occurring daily on the earth.

-Archangel Sebastian

NEAR DEATH EXPERIENCES (NDE)

The most common type of miracle, as viewed on earth, is when a person escapes the threshold of death. But what is death on the human side? Death on earth is viewed as a complete shutdown of a person's body...all the major organs cease to function such that the body of the human being is no longer able to exist on earth.

What is death on the spiritual side? Death on the spiritual side is a rebirth of the soul. With death, the soul returns to its origin or home having completed its tasks on earth.

Now, there are many who have crossed the barrier between earth and heaven with the intent of staying in heaven, but we angels were able to stop the process and return those souls to earth because it was not their time to transition to heaven.

What happened?

How was that possible?

Let's look behind the scenes with the angels for a spiritual explanation of the miracles that are witnessed on earth.

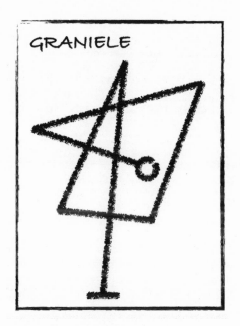

GRANIELE

I am Archangel Graniele and I recently assisted guardian angels return a middle-aged man to earth before he completely came over to our side.

The young man was in construction work and was always aware of the dangers of his job. Each morning he would kiss his wife and baby daughter goodbye with the promise that he would return in the evening. On one particular morning, the weather turned bad with rain and fog surrounding the construction project that he was working on. The construction team became aware of the bad weather but believed they had about an hour before they needed to stop their work. They decided they had enough time to attach another support beam to the bridge they were repairing. All on the team were aware of the impending danger from the rain and fog. They purposely moved slowly and with caution to secure the support beam to the bridge high above the water.

Without warning, the workers suddenly felt the scaffolding, on which they were standing, starting to sway. The group on the ground saw, in what seemed to be slow motion, the collapse of the scaffolding and four members of their team plunging into the icy water. The ground team rushed to the water's edge as they called 911 for help. They were able to pull three workers to the shore. The fourth worker was further out in the water and looked to be unconscious. The sirens could be heard in the distance as the workers continued frantically to try to rescue the fourth worker.

The emergency crew rescued the young worker from the water and quickly transported him to the nearest hospital. On the way to the hospital, the rescue team recorded that his heart stopped beating two times.

The hospital team whisked him away quickly and efficiently, calling out stats and hooking him to IV's. The construction worker's heart suddenly stopped beating. When his other organs began to slow significantly, the emergency staff stopped working and removed their masks. A heart beep suddenly echoed from the heart monitor. They immediately returned to the patient but this time they did not have to do anything. They all stood there and watched as his heart became stronger and his breathing returned to normal.

What happened, the staff asked each other? This man was truly dead and now he is alive. One doctor stated that this was another 'miracle' from God. He had witnessed these miraculous happenings several times while working in the emergency room. This man has been given another chance at life, he said. I hope he uses it wisely.

Shortly after the young construction worker's miraculous recovery in the emergency room, the attending physician came to his bedside. He looked at the young worker and told him that he was 'kicked' back to earth because his soul was not ready…that he should look at his life, long and hard, and be grateful for the opportunity to live his life again knowing the angels are with him all the way.

As the construction worker recovered in the hospital, he related many times how he knew he died because he saw a blinding light and heard beautiful music. He said he wanted to stay, but the voices he heard told him that he must return to earth. It was his choice to stay or return, he said, but the voices were very strong urging him to go back to earth.

His family and friends were ecstatic to hear of his recovery. They listened very intently to his 'near death' experience with heaven and the angels. Many stated that he was told to come back for a reason and that he had better search his soul for the answer. He thought about that for a while, remembering the words of the physician from the emergency room, but he was so happy to see his wife and daughter again, he put off looking inside himself to search for the true reason for his new life.

This jubilation and awe represent the human perspective of a near-death 'miracle'. Now let's look at what was occurring on the spiritual side.

I helped prepare this soul for his journey to earth, so I had a vested interest that he be successful in completing his life plan. He was moving through life at a very nice pace always trying to be aware of his life and his feelings for others. He was strong physically and spiritually. He was extremely independent and was very happy with his life just prior to the accident.

Now the accident was written into his life plan because he wanted to experience the feeling of needing others to help him physically. While the accident was occurring, we angels watched very carefully. As he lay in the water, his soul cried out that he didn't know if he could continue with this accident. His body was hurt badly. His soul wanted to return to us. His soul called out that it needed more time and training with us angels to be able to continue with this accident and with life.

We watched as he came closer and closer to us until he was able to see our auras. His spirit could see us because he was disconnecting from his body. I knew he was strong enough for this earthly experience but fear engulfed him and this was an opportunity for him to return to us. His guardian angels, many archangels and myself loudly told him to go back. He had only a few seconds remaining to choose to stay with us or return to his body. Any split-second hesitation in that period and his soul would have completely transitioned to be with us in heaven. We shouted again and descended upon him with an extremely bright light. He said 'okay' and we immediately helped him return to his body.

We imprinted on his mind the experience of being present with us. We wanted him to remember that he saw our auras and heard our voices and that he CHOSE to return to earth,

Now we angels watched as he progressed in the hospital. He talked incessantly to everyone about the 'voices' he heard and the 'bright light' that intensified right before he returned to his body. We were happy that he remembered his experience with us and hoped that he would use this memory as he continued his journey on earth.

Now, let's fast-forward in this man's life. The accident left him disabled. He was able to walk slowly but painfully due to the injuries in his back. Since he was unable to do construction work, he studied and became proficient in computer software repair. His reputation grew in this field so that he was able to open a business and support his family. He worked from his home because he was unable to drive due to limited mobility and pain in his legs. He related his near-death experience many times to his customers when he first established his computer business but as time moved on he spoke less and less of this event. We could see that he was becoming agitated with his disabled body. He questioned himself as to 'why' he returned. He was starting to believe that he should have died in the accident.

'What kind of life do I have now', he would say to his wife. She could see that he was starting to give up and feared that he would try to end his life. She remembered how strongly he spoke of the angels when he was in the hospital so she called on us to help her give him the strength he needed to accept his life and disability.

While at home one morning and feeling sorry for himself, the young man tripped and fell to the floor. No one was there to help him. He was not able to get up. He banged his fists on the floor until they started to bleed. At this point, he put his head down and with tears in his eyes cried out for us angels to come and help him. He screamed that we helped him when he was dying so please come help him now.

A postman had just walked onto the porch to deliver a package. We instructed the postman to ring the bell and as he reached for the button he heard a call for help within the house. The postman opened the unlocked door and walked in. He immediately went to the fallen man and called 911 for he could see that the young man had injured his head and shoulder.

We angels accompanied him to the hospital. His soul did not try to return to us this time. However, we knew that his soul had become frustrated with its life just before the fall. As we comforted and encouraged his soul to continue with its life on earth, his soul communicated that it was willing to try to stay focused on its present life. We reminded the soul that the physical difficulties were written in its life plan.

The attending physician in the emergency room recognized the young man as the construction worker whom he had treated during his near-death experience. The physician introduced himself again and told the young man that he was glad to see that he was doing so well with his life since the accident. 'Consider yourself very lucky', the physician said. 'You apparently are here to experience a great lesson and to spread your knowledge about the angels and heaven's doorstep to those who cross your path'.

The young man's wife was present when the physician said these words to her husband. She immediately knew the angels had heard her requests to help her open her husband's eyes for the reason behind his disabled life.

My message to you is to always be aware of why you are here on earth. Are you here to experience a physical difficulty, a personal tragedy, or are you here to be a caregiver to your family or to strangers?

BE AWARE OF YOUR LIFE.

Don't feel sorry for yourself. Look around and see where you can spread love and happiness.

Remember, there are always many who are in more difficult situations than you… recognize, reach out and extend your helping hand no matter how crippled it may be.

-Archangel Graniele

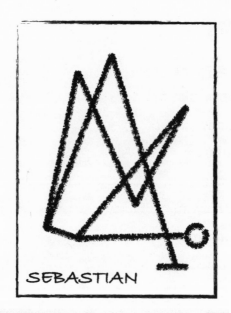

SEBASTIAN

A Near-Death Experience does not always mean that a heart stops in the emergency room, and a soul visualizes a white light while hearing beautiful music.

I am Archangel Sebastian and I would like to tell you about a little girl who was born with a defective gene. The altered gene rendered the girl almost incapacitated with seizures. Now seizures, in infants and children, are currently well understood and most hospitals are able to help their young patients.

This little girl experienced very small seizures as an infant. Her parents and physician did not recognize these small seizures during her infant and toddler years. The seizures remained non-descript until she was about four years old. The parents then noticed a change in her behavior...a sudden 'zoning' out... not able to hear or respond to any verbal communication. The parents were alarmed when they saw this but were relieved when she returned to her happy self within a minute. The second seizure of this nature occurred about three weeks later and for a longer period of time. The seizures progressed until the little girl 'zoned out' for over an hour. The parents immediately rushed their little girl to the children's hospital in their city. Upon examining the little girl, the doctors were very concerned with this behavior pattern. However, following an MRI, the doctors were confident with the diagnosis that the 'zoning out' was definitely seizure related. The little girl was prescribed medication with routine follow-up visits and medical tests.

The parents were satisfied with this diagnosis and the little girl was allowed to returned to school. All went well for this family for approximately one year. The little girl then had a seizure similar to the previous ones but this one was more intense. The parents called 911 for they could see the little girl was starting to have trouble breathing.

At the hospital, the emergency nurses and doctors worked feverishly to save the little girl. Suddenly a calm descended over the emergency room where the little girl lay on the table. All of the attending staff could hear soft music although no one in the room said what they felt or heard. All of them were able to see a light beaming into the little girl. It encompassed her entire body. The medical team stopped immediately somehow knowing a higher source was working on the little girl. When the light subsided, the medical team returned to the patient.

When the little girl awoke, she was very alert and happy. She told her parents that she had been playing with her angels. She said it was fun and everything there was beautiful with trees, and flowers and lots of toys. She said that she liked being there. Her angels told her when it was time for her to go home to her parents. They told me that 'you were waiting for me'. The parents cried when their little girl talked of her angel experience because they knew that she was with them in heaven.

The 'miracle' in the hospital was intended for this particular medical staff.

The little girl had continued experiencing seizures until the right medical staff was gathered together to treat her in the emergency department. It was intended that they experience the presence of a higher source. This attending medical staff had progressed to a level of believing that they were solely responsible for saving human lives. It was necessary to show them the presence of the TRUE healing source that guided them each and every day in the emergency room.

Did this medical group respond intellectually or spiritually to what they witnessed?

They gathered together when the little girl transitioned to the recovery room. Several on this medical team questioned what had just occurred. It was spiritual, one doctor exclaimed, while another said that it was a faulty light in the room and that they were the ones who did all the work. Several of the other doctors and nurses just stood there in awe and listened, trying to make sense of the event. Another emergency came in and they dispersed to where they were needed.

Now the experience with the little girl did not have an immediate effect on the healthcare workers but it was imprinted in their memory. As they progressed through life, several recalled this event when they witnessed similar healings in the emergency room. They acknowledged immediately to themselves that the healings were not totally a result of their personal skills.

In summary, this little girl incarnated to earth to help other souls open their hearts to see the light of God. She helped this hospital team reunite with their souls so they would be able to see the true reason for their presence on earth.

It was important for each of them to realize that as healthcare professionals they are guided to help others only through the hands of God.

-Archangel Sebastian

We could go on and on describing 'near death' experiences. Humans are always in awe of the details of these types of events. They like to hear and remember these stories because many times they feel the love of God and the angels when the stories are told to them. And that is good because we are always sending our love to earth and we are very happy when it is received. Unfortunately, many see only the human side of the story and not the spiritual side. They acknowledge how wonderful the 'miracle' must have been for the person who experienced it and they are happy that a soul was able to stay on earth and not die.

First, to all those who 'hear' the details of these ND experiences, we want you to expand your mind to look beyond the human part of the phenomenon. Turn your mind to the soul of the person who experienced the event and then turn your mind to your soul. As you experience the feeling of happiness for the person's ND survival, think first that the soul was returned to earth because its life plan (which was written before it incarnated) was not complete. This soul has more work to do on earth before it returns to God. Now, that is all we want you to think about concerning the other soul because it is not up to you to figure out why it survived and what it needs to accomplish to complete its life plan.

We want you to think about your life and your soul.

You have just read of a ND experience of another soul and you are probably glad that it did not happen to you. No, you did not experience the physical event but we angels brought this story TO you for a reason. Think about that! By bringing this story to you, we are sending you messages to become aware of your life. We are telling you to become aware of your soul and your soul development. You are here for specific experiences that are designed to grow your soul closer to God.

Look at your life. Evaluate your life. Determine if your soul is in alignment with God.

In summary, 'near death' experiences are true miracles when ALL who are involved look inward to their souls and truly realize that they have been given a sign or message directly from God. The true miracle continues when all those souls who have been touched by a miracle reach out to us angels for direction and help.

-Archangel Sebastian

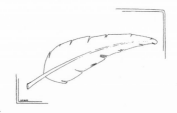

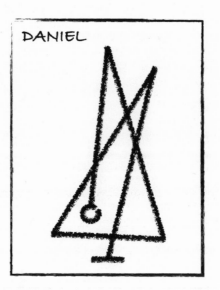

DANIEL

CANCER

The cancer virus is rampant on earth today and many people personally witness 'miracle cures' of their relatives and friends. Miraculous cures are also reported on television and social media of those who have recovered from very aggressive cancer attacks.

Fear of this virus is pervasive on earth. Reports of increased scientific studies and increased positive results have lifted the spirits of many who fear cancer will invade their bodies. Many also believe that because the virus existed in their family tree, they are immediately susceptible to the virus and wait fearfully through the years for their doctors to give them the doomsday cancer information.

The most fearful occurrence of cancer is with children. These young souls are viewed as totally innocent and should never be subject to a childhood full of hardship. Bundles of prayers come our way to remove this illness from children. We angels are asked to pass the cancer on to the adults who are sending us petitions because they feel they have already lived and experienced life. They want the little children who have cancer to live a life that is free from suffering.

Many see the cancer virus as evil. They believe that God is punishing them for past wrongdoings. Because of their cancer, they feel they have failed God and this is His retribution. Depression and self-disappointment become part of their persona as they experience the cancer virus.

Facing the unknown with a virus raging war on one's body and the fear of leaving the known (earth) and going to the unknown (heaven) is definitely frightening. We angels see and understand these feelings. We know how everyone with cancer wants and prays desperately for a 'miracle cure' for this virus. Prayers are full of petitions to remove this virus completely from the human race.

-Archangel Daniel

Now, let's explore the cancer 'miracle cures'.

The cancer unit in the hospital always bustled with activity. There are patients making their way to their favorite seats for their chemotherapy infusions. Many, with smiles and upbeat personalities, greet the medical staff. The staff, at this hospital, has witnessed several 'miracle cures' and is always in awe when it happens. One particular cure is mentioned almost daily even though it occurred over a year ago. The patient was in her mid-thirties and had contracted a rare form of cancer that invaded her lower back. Her physique was physically strong when the virus entered her body because she was an avid runner and athlete. When she experienced pain in her lower back and legs, she shrugged it off to a grueling physical workout. However, when she started to lose her balance from weak legs, she sought the advice of her doctor. Following many medical tests, nothing could be found. The patient was then directed to see a physical therapist for a possible muscle or ligament injury. The young girl persisted with the therapy but did not see any improvement. Her body became weaker and she developed a fear of falling from her unstable legs. This was heartbreaking for her because she loved to run and compete in marathon events.

Her cancer was finally diagnosed but not until it had progressed significantly throughout her spine. She was devastated when she received the results of the medical tests. The doctors did not have much hope to offer her because her cancer was so rare. There were only a few studies for the doctors to refer to for a treatment plan for this patient. Several said they would like to work with her with the understanding that all the procedures would be experimental.

The young girl was competitive and ready to fight for a cure not only for herself but also for others who might contract this type of cancer virus. She sought the opinions of several well-respected and highly advanced cancer physicians. They were all interested in her case and agreed with her oncologists that all of her treatments would be new and experimental. She accepted the challenge the doctors set before her... she knew she was in for the 'run' of her life.

We angels surrounded her daily sending her love and support as she progressed through the steps of her chemo treatment. She was strong for her friends and medical staff but inside we saw her crying.

'Why me, God'?

'What did I do to deserve this'?

'Are you there, God'?

'I think you have walked away from me and I don't understand why'.

She cried these words every night in the solitude of her bedroom. She was very angry at this time and turned away from us angels and from God. We tried to send her messages but her heart slammed shut for any spiritual communication. We angels never gave up. In fact, we intensified our love, our messages and our signs to her.

When she started the chemo infusions, she walked into the room deliberately and with confidence. We angels were happy to see her show of strength. She understood the treatment process was going to be long and arduous. So, week after week, the medical staff signed her in and interacted with small talk because they sensed that she was very distraught even though she tried to hide it. As the treatments continued, she became weaker and weaker. The doctors were fearful her cancer was not responding to the drugs as they had anticipated. We angels stepped in at this time and directed her oncologist to a national conference regarding the occurrence of rare cancers and possible treatments. Her physician attended the conference and received the information he needed to develop another treatment plan for this young patient.

A very good friend visited the young girl and was shocked at her mental state. As a fellow runner, her friend immediately gave her a pep talk similar to the ones they would give to each other before a marathon run. She asked the young girl to remember their supporting words to each other before each marathon that they had run together. She asked the young girl to recite them. The young girl shook her head and whispered that she could not. She told her friend that she was running out of energy. She said her energy level now is the lowest she has ever experienced after any race, even after the grueling mountain race. The young friend saw the desperate and tired look in the young girl's eyes. 'Please don't give up now', she whispered with tears in her eyes. 'I know the angels will direct your doctors'. The young girl answered that she believed that God had abandoned her completely.

She said to her friend…LOOK AT ME…I AM A MESS. 'I was so strong and I believed I was leading a productive life'.

Her friend responded that maybe God had other intentions for her…that she may be slated for a more significant role in life. The young girl just sat quietly contemplating the words her friend had just said.

At the next meeting with her oncology team, the young girl was a little more hopeful but still ready to throw in the towel and let the cancer take control of her body. Her team explained, in detail, the new drugs and regimens they had learned about at the recent cancer symposium. There was one study in progress that they were particularly interested in for this young girl. She listened carefully but grew very hesitant and fearful when they explained the particulars involved in the drug regimen. The drug would be administered in the hospital over a three-day constant infusion with a ten-day rest period. Eight cycles would be involved with this procedure. The side effects would be brutal but if she could endure they believed she would be cancer free.

We angels watched as she struggled with her decision to try yet another cancer regimen. If she decided to let the cancer take over her body, she would be received over here with open arms and love. If she decided to continue on earth to combat her cancer, we would be by her side supporting, helping, guiding and loving her.

Her friends visited her daily, encouraging her to fight for a new life. She wanted to 'throw in the towel' right now, she told them, because she was so very tired. She said she was tired not only from the physical effects of the chemo drugs but also spiritually. She was tired of praying her heart out and getting no response. She said she felt abandoned by God and His angels.

The young girl made the decision to try this regimen with the doctors. She prepared herself for the side effects as best she could. The first two infusion rounds were brutal on her body.

She lay in the hospital bed hardly able to move or even breathe. She took a deep breath at the start of the third infusion and with tears in her eyes, she whispered to those around her that she was very tired and didn't think she would make it through this infusion.

Three days post her third infusion, her soul returned to us. As we prepared for her arrival, we kept talking to her, asking if she absolutely wanted to transition over to us. She responded yes because she believed she was abandoned by God while on earth. We let her come very close to us angels so that she could see us and feel our love. God then came to her and wrapped His arms around her soul. She was divinely engulfed in God's love.

She asked Him, 'why didn't you hear me on earth'?

He responded that He was closer to her than she could ever imagine but her fear kept Him out of her heart. He encouraged the young girl to return to earth to finish her life plan as it was written before she incarnated to earth. He told her that if she returned to earth she would recover in order to help others understand their difficult experiences with cancer and to bring His love to them.

There was a flurry of activity in the chemo area with this young girl as the doctors and nurses saw her slipping away.

She was immediately transferred to the hospital intensive care unit. The attending staff worked feverishly to save her life and stepped away as they saw all her vital signs quickly slip to zero. The doctors removed their masks and as they opened their mouths to pronounce that her heart had stopped and the other organs were shutting down quickly they saw her monitors signaling that she was coming back.

There was great elation when she was moved from the intensive care unit to a hospital room and finally discharged.

The young girl did not receive any more of the new chemo drug or any other chemo treatments. After many exhausting tests, the doctors declared that she was free of all cancer cells. The young girl then knew for sure that her 'vision' with God, while in the hospital, had truly occurred. She was very thankful to God for her 'miracle' and related her story to as many people as she could.

As she recalled her 'vision', she remembered the reason why she returned to earth...to work with cancer patients to help remove their fear of the disease and to recognize the special love that surrounds them. This special love is from God and His angels.

This event is a true miracle because the person's soul left its body and traveled over to us.

The soul received special words of comfort and instruction from us angels and from God.

This soul heeded our words of encouragement and completed its time on earth helping others remove their fear of cancer and receive God into their hearts.

-Archangel Daniel

ANGELOSE

CHILDHOOD CANCER

Babies, toddlers, children and even teens with cancer are heartbreaking to see and hear about on the news or read about on Facebook. These souls are very strong souls to agree to experience the cancer virus at a young age when they incarnate to earth.

Many of these souls receive the virus to help educate researchers and physicians in their studies to understand, treat and hopefully eradicate cancer. Some children take on the virus to help other souls open their closed hearts to God. And there are those souls who want to bring God's love directly to the medical staff whom they will be working with.

So, when you see a child with cancer, don't just look with tears in your eyes and say 'why the little ones, God'?

Look deeply into the hearts of these children and try to understand the 'why' behind their receiving the virus.

Talk to teenagers who have had or presently have cancer and you will see a totally different perspective on life.

Children are not angry and they have little fear of cancer. Some are disappointed that they are unable to participate in many activities with their friends but this disappointment is usually a driving force for them to continue their fight to heal their bodies.

They are not afraid to return to us. Parents are the ones who are afraid. They are afraid of losing their child and rightly so.

-Archangel Angelose

Let me show you how children with cancer understand life on earth.

The ten-year-old boy was the 'apple' of his grandmother's eyes. He was athletic, friendly, good-looking, happy, and a joy to be around. He loved his grandmother and visited her often. He would sit with her for hours. They loved to read books together, play games together and watch their favorite shows on television. They had a very special relationship. The day his grandmother received the news that her grandson was diagnosed with a rare form of leukemia, she cried all day. Her immediate thoughts were about her and how lonely she would be without her grandson. Her daughter tried to console her mother by saying that she and her husband were seeking several opinions for the best treatment for the little boy.

Following many rounds of chemotherapy, interspersed with rest time for his body to heal, the little athlete became very weak but his spirits soared. He always believed God was with him in the hospital. His mother and grandmother visited him in the hospital every day. Many times, when they approached his room, they heard him faintly laughing and talking. They expected to see a nurse or doctor in the room but when they entered, no one was there.

'Who were you talking with', his mother would ask as she approached his bed?

'Some friends here in the hospital', he responded, 'didn't you see them'?

His grandmother and mother both shook their heads and said they saw no one leave his room.

His parents had many meetings with their son's doctors and learned the leukemia was going into remission. Their child would heal but it would be a slow process and they were warned the cancer could return at any time. The medical group would monitor him closely. They said that the little boy was exhausted but his spirit was dynamic. They loved going into his room because it was so uplifting and filled with love.

The little boy returned home to recover and spread the news that his friends from the hospital would come to visit him. When no one came, his parents and grandmother were concerned. They did not want to see the little boy disappointed.

Then one day, they heard him talking and laughing as he played by himself in his bedroom. His mother, father and grandmother ran up the steps and into his bedroom. As they peeked around the entry to his room, they could see his face shining with love as he laughed and talked.

'Who is he playing with', they whispered to each other?

'Imaginary friends' was the answer, they decided.

So, they walked in and asked about his 'friends'. The little boy just gleamed when he told his parents and grandmother that God had sent him some angels to keep him company while he was sick. 'They always make me feel good', he told them. They said that God was very proud of me because I was able to show the doctors a new form of cancer and they could learn how to treat me and be prepared to help other people when they get it. He turned back to his 'imaginary friends', the angels, and giggled and laughed as he continued his conversation with them.

The little boy's health returned. He was able to go back to school and participate in all the activities he had previously enjoyed. His grandmother was delighted when he walked through the threshold of her front door. It's over, she sighed; the terrible nightmare of losing my grandson is over. I will see him graduate from high school and college and hopefully see him get married. She talked of nothing else to her friends. The little boy, her grandson, was her life.

The little boy's medical team was overwhelmed with his blood work that supported a diagnosis of a full recovery. They did not expect to see the positive results so soon after his chemotherapy treatments. They had believed that this type of cancer would be resistant to the experimental drugs that they had tried. They knew that the traditional chemo drugs for this type of cancer would not work so they felt forced to try the new chemo drugs.

But how long would his recovery last, they asked themselves? They all had their doubts because they knew very little about the experimental drugs. They kept the little boy on a tight monitoring schedule because of their fears. Each month when the little boy came in for his blood work and visit with the doctors, he could see through the stern look on their faces that they were worried. He was not worried because the angels had told the little boy that all the cancer cells were removed from his body. He tried to tell the doctors that he was really okay but they believed that he did not understand the gravity of his cancer. When he told them that he got his information from the angels, they just smiled and said, 'that's nice'.

At that point he knew they did not believe him, so he stood up and looked them straight in the eyes and asked, 'DO YOU BELIEVE IN GOD, DO YOU BELIEVE IN ANGELS'?

The boy continued to say that it was God who got rid of the cancer cells and the angels worked with God.

The little boy then said loudly and clearly that it was 'GOD WHO DIRECTED YOU, THE MEDICAL TEAM, TO THE NEW CHEMO DRUGS'.

'I became infected with the cancer cells to help YOU find the drugs needed for this disease. It will help all the children after me', he said.

The medical team just sat there and looked at the little boy. He was ten years old yet he spoke like a college graduate. They thanked the little boy for this information and left the room.

The boy's parents were in awe of their son and knew then that they had just witnessed a miracle.

Their son was not afraid of the disease and he was not afraid of dying because he knew that he was on a special mission for God. He came to earth to educate the medical staff about how God works through children to show the researchers and doctors the path to help eradicate the many diseases afflicting mankind today.

-Archangel Angelose

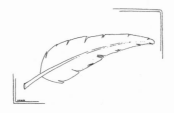

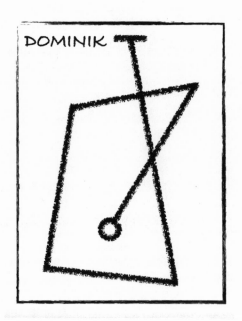

ADDICTION

Everyone on earth has addictions. There are addictions to coffee where it HAS to be a certain brand, type and temperature. There are addictions to desserts, chocolate, exercise, and the list goes on and on.

Addictions can be good if you are 'addicted' to the spirit world of God and His angels.

Addictions can be bad if they interrupt the flow of your written plan for your life on earth.

Once you move away from your written plan, you move away from God.

Once you move away from God, you move away from your soul development process on earth.

Once you move away from developing your soul, you stop all the processes that have been put into place to guide you through your experiences on earth.

Addiction to drugs is the most identifiable type of addiction. The news reports from around the world are resplendent with the horrors of drug addictions not only to young people, but also to the affluent, to the poor, to academia, to businesses, and to all races of people in all countries.

Addiction to drugs is not the only deleterious addiction on earth. There is obsessive-compulsion addiction, self-destruction addiction, child pornography addiction, prejudice-hate addiction, cruelty addiction, and many, many more. Where there is a repetitive destructive behavior, there is addiction.

Destructive addictions must be recognized, stopped and the soul must return its actions to its written plan in order to return to God. This is not an easy task for any level of addiction but we angels surround the addicted person. We work with them constantly to bring them back to God. We send our messengers to intervene. We surround them with a massive amount of love and we talk to them constantly. Many times, our voices are shunned because they believe that it is their conscience coming through and they don't want to feel guilty each time they succumb to their addiction.

Let me give you a few examples of some souls who have moved miraculously through their addictive personalities. It is important that you observe how strong the pull an addiction can have on a person and the strength that is needed to overcome a harmful habit.

-Archangel Dominik

Let's look at the drug epidemic first. It is the addiction that most people are aware of, because of its far-reaching destructive ability. It reaches into all levels of society, from the very poor and uneducated to those who are very rich and successful.

I will first tell you of a young girl, under my guidance, who was very well liked and popular in high school. She received awards that recognized her volunteer work with senior citizens in her community. Her personality bristled with energy and happiness. She excelled academically and received a scholarship to a well-known university.

As she progressed through college, she found many diverse students with whom she loved to converse to learn about their cultures. She visited the homes of several of her student friends and noted how different their lives were, compared to hers, even though they all lived in the same country.

It was through several of these friends that she learned about many drugs that are so easily available on the streets. She was aware of the drugs but only at a distance and had absolutely no desire to try any type of drug. However, her personality was such that she never wanted to disappoint anyone. When she was offered a rolled drug to smoke, she panicked because she did not want to say 'no' to her new friend. She wanted to just run to get out of the situation. She nervously said that she did not 'smoke' and excused herself to go to her room and study for a test. Upon returning to the dorm, she locked her door, and cried. She was afraid. She was afraid because she felt she had blinded herself from the real environment around her. She felt like a 'goody two-shoes'. She looked to see the good in everyone and refused to listen to the warnings of her true friends about some of the college kids that she had recently befriended.

Her parents were very proud of their daughter when she graduated college. She was immediately hired as a junior journalist for a well-known newspaper. Being a journalist was perfect for this young girl because she loved to meet and talk to people and she loved to travel. The position was demanding with time-lines and deadlines. She worked feverishly every day and many nights to complete her assignments. This hard work was not in vain for she started to move up in the world of journalism. Soon, she was given special assignments on high profile cases. She traveled internationally for interviews important for her reports. Her world became busier and busier, typing while sitting in airports, on planes and even late at night in her hotel room.

A few of her co-workers noticed how feverishly she worked and that she never joined them for any social activities. They shrugged this off at first knowing she was 'new' in the field and that she wanted to make a good impression with her bosses. They admired her for her tenacity to stay with her stories even when they were not very exciting or interesting but necessary.

She always smiled and was very friendly to her co-reporters but suddenly they noticed a change in her. She lost the 'bounce' in her walk and her smiles were very weak. Her eyes became sallow. Her friends became very concerned with the physical decline of this young reporter. They observed her closely when she stood in front of the television monitors and used every ounce of energy that she had to perform with a smile on her face.

Then the day came when she did not report to work. There were no phone calls to anyone in the newsroom nor to any of her friends. They immediately knew something was wrong. Several left the office and headed for her condominium...there was no answer when they knocked on her door. They kept banging loudly with their fists. A nearby tenant came into the hallway. They asked this gentleman if he knew the young girl who lived in the condominium where they were knocking on the door. He verified that he did know her and loved the happy smile on her face each time he saw her. She didn't come home last night, he said. The reason that I know this is because my wife and I had planned to take her to dinner to celebrate her birthday. The young girl's friends thanked the gentleman and left.

As they walked down the street, they saw what looked like blood on the sidewalk that trailed into a deserted street. Being reporters, they followed the trail of blood. Walking briskly down this street, they observed many needles and drug paraphernalia. Then they found their friend. She was passed out next to a building with blood still oozing from her arm and leg. They stayed with her until the emergency crew arrived.

The young girl started in the drug scene with prescription sleeping pills. As the demands of her job increased, she increased the number of pills to help her sleep. Through her many assignments of interviewing and reporting on drug related deaths and accidents, she knew where to go for more potent drugs to help her sleep. She believed that she would be okay because she was taking them only to help her sleep and not for the pleasure of getting 'high'. This pattern continued for about one year and she felt she had her life under control. Then she started waking up in the middle of the night and this caused her to take more drugs. The people who supplied her with the drugs told her that her body had built a tolerance to the drug that she was taking and that she should try some cocaine. This was the beginning of the end for this beautiful, successful and intelligent young girl.

By the time her friends discovered her in the cocaine overdose, she was already moving close to us angels. It was not her time to return to us and we needed to imprint on her soul the gravity of her actions. She knowingly and carelessly walked down a path in life that could destroy her. She incarnated to earth for the purpose of helping those struggling with life by directing them to the necessary resources that they needed to start a new life. Her work in journalism was perfect for her to identify and bring to the public's attention the needs of the less fortunate. She blew it and we needed to slow her ascent to this realm and give her another chance to complete her written plan for this incarnation.

By the time the ambulance arrived, her pulse rate and bodily functions were seriously low. We supported the ambulance crew as well as the staff in the emergency room. As she came closer to us, we let her see our auras and faces. We wanted her to remember this peaceful moment. We held her hands and urged her gently to return to earth. She said it was very hard down there. She said that she wanted to stay with us. She wanted to feel our love at this level forever. She said she couldn't feel or hear us on earth. We told her that she had turned away from us when she chose to make the mind-altering drugs her life.

'With drugs, your mind is dulled and you are unable to connect with us angels. Drugs take you farther and farther away from reality, from God and from us', we said.

'Go back to earth now. Remember our words. Remember we are always with you no matter how difficult life may appear to you, however, you MUST ask us for direction and help'.

She was coming closer and closer to us not wanting to return to earth. Michael Archangel came forward just then and with his strong voice he told the young girl that she had a purpose on earth and it was necessary to return so that she could help the people who contributed to her demise. She was to show them how to open their minds and hearts to God and imprint on them that they also have specific jobs on earth that must be completed before they return to God.

'Know that I will always walk with you, for this will be a very powerful task for you to undertake. Call on me and talk to me EVERY day for you will become a soldier in my army to fight the war on drugs', Michael Archangel strongly stated.

The young girl responded immediately to Michael Archangel's message and asked for our help to return to earth. The staff in the hospital room had already removed their gloves and started to move on to the next patient believing the young girl had died. As she was being prepped to move out of the emergency room and to the hospital morgue, a nurse saw movement in the young girl's closed eyes. She hollered loudly for help and immediately began hooking the young girl's body to the heart monitor. The machine beeped softly at first and steadily increased. We walked with her, holding her hands as her soul returned to her body.

Now this young girl returned to the earth realm and healed very quickly. She related her spiritual visit with us angels to as many people who would listen to her. She clearly remembered the words of Michael Archangel and knew she was receiving a lot of help from the 'other side'. She was very enthusiastic to start her new mission in life.

During her recovery period, she studied the plethora of street drugs and learned how far they reached into the societies of the world. She realized then the enormity of drug addictions in the world as well as the enormity of her new mission in life.

We stayed very close to the young girl at this stage of her life knowing that she might again decide to walk away from this new life.

She struggled to stay 'clean', but unfortunately, she slipped several times returning to her favorite drugs.

As she lay in a drunken stupor one afternoon, Michael Archangel walked up to her and shook her awake. She was immediately frightened with this stranger shaking her and preaching to her. When he touched her hand to help her stand up, she immediately moved out of her stupor and felt love radiating throughout her body. She was not afraid anymore.

When he reminded her of her near-death experience, she suddenly remembered meeting Michael Archangel. She then looked at him directly when he said '*Remember Me*'.

He turned and walked away as memories filled her mind of her encounter with angels and in particular, Michael Archangel.

This second meeting with Michael gave her the strength to pull herself up from the depths of drugs.

She recalled her meetings with Michael Archangel every day to remind herself why she had incarnated to earth.

She slowly grew stronger and with the help of the angels she worked to expose and inform the world of the drug infestation that is thriving on earth.

-Archangel Dominik

Working with those addicted to drugs is a very difficult and slow process. The addict will take two steps forward and the counselor is ecstatic seeing possible progress. Then the addict takes four steps back. Drugs are very difficult for an addicted person to give up.

Drugs give the human body comfort and a shield when a soul becomes frightened and overwhelmed with life. That is why those who try to walk away from drugs run right back to them. They are afraid of the demands of life. They are afraid to succeed, they are afraid of not being accepted by friends, and they are afraid of themselves.

Life can appear to be demanding but the demands of life are often self-imposed.

Life is not difficult when you trust that we angels are walking with you. When you walk away and forget about us, fear enters into your life. When fear enters into your life, your soul may then start wandering away from its written path searching for answers to calm its fears.

Many times, drugs are found to be THE answer to calm all fears.

Many times, it takes a 'MIRACLE' to break the drug addiction cycle and bring one back to his written path in life.

-Archangel Dominik

ALCOHOL ADDICTION

Alcohol abuse and addiction have been present in all societies of the world for thousands of years. Since it is an accepted 'drug', it is readily available to the old as well as to the young, and to the rich as well as to the poor.

It is as popular in today's society as it was in biblical times as recorded in history books. I am not condemning the use of alcohol. Humans have consumed it wisely for a very long time. I want to focus on the abuse and the addiction to alcohol.

Many cultures have embraced alcohol in their family settings. Children receive small amounts for a toast on special occasions. Other cultures prohibit children from receiving any type of alcohol until a certain age. No matter the circumstances of when a person receives his first taste of alcohol, it is the desire to continue its consumption that could be harmful especially if it interferes with their life's plan thus causing their soul to move away from God.

Alcohol abuse causes harm not only to the human body but also to all the people who surround and love the addicted person.

We angels have assisted in developing many alcohol recovery programs. As messengers of God, we help direct many souls to these programs. It is very important that a person, addicted to alcohol, receive help because if they spend their life in a drunken stupor they are wasting their time on earth. They are accomplishing nothing in the way of developing their soul. They have totally walked away from their written contract with God.

Our goal is to awaken these addicted souls to their destructive behavior, rehabilitate them and move them back onto their written plan with God.

-Archangel Dominik

I, Archangel Dominik, personally visited the earth realm to assist the recovery and rehabilitation of an old man who had spent the majority of his life on earth drinking and partying.

The young boy started drinking beer when he was about twelve years old. Initially, he would just take sips from his father's glass. He liked the taste. By the time the boy graduated from high school, he usually drank a couple bottles of beer with his friends on weekends.

His parents were elated when the young man announced that he wanted to go to college to study engineering. However, by the end of his second year in college, the young man had reduced his studies to two courses each semester so that he could have more time to party and drink.

He was fun to be around and easily found parties on campus. He was able to drink a fair amount of beer and still appear sober. His friends were in awe of his beer-drinking level. He liked this attention from his friends and was very proud of his alcohol capacity.

However, his first accident came following a weekend party where he assured everyone that he was still sober and was quite capable of driving. He strolled casually and with confidence to his car to begin his drive back to campus. Along the way he started to feel drowsy. When he awoke from his drunken stupor, he was in the emergency room of the local hospital with doctors and several police officers. He learned that he had driven his car into a tree on a very sharp turn. He just missed going down a steep embankment that would have caused serious injury.

His parents rushed to the hospital upon receiving news of their son's accident. They were very happy that his injuries were minimal. When the police addressed the DUI charge their son would receive, they were in shock. They had no idea. They told the police their son was an engineering student at the university and had little time to party and drink. The police advised the parents to talk to their son and investigate his drinking habit.

The young boy knew he was 'busted' when his parents found out about his partying, drinking and reduced class schedule. He refused to believe that he could have died in his car accident when he was drunk. His parents told him that he must graduate with the engineering degree within four years. They stated they would not pay any more money for education past that time. He promised to change his habits and return to a heavy class schedule to catch up. He also promised that he would not touch alcohol while in school. They believed him and were happy as they left the hospital.

They young boy returned to school with a renewed heart. He worked to catch up on his missed classes but he was really missing the party scene. His parents sent many reminders for him to stay straight. He tried very hard but the call of the alcohol was strong. He would have a couple of beers on weekends after studying but soon these couple of beers increased to five, six, and even seven or eight. He was slipping again. He liked the relaxed feeling he got with alcohol.

We angels were watching very carefully now, because he was descending into the realm of alcoholism very quickly. We sent him many signs and messages. We tried to surround him with friends who would support his efforts to stay sober but he moved away from them quickly. He was tired of hearing their warnings on the dangers of drinking. They tried to encourage his success in engineering and tell him how brilliant he was. That made him think of his parents and how he didn't want to disappoint them but he pushed those thoughts out of his head for another beer. Gradually, all of his college friends drifted away from him. He was not 'fun' anymore. He was just a 'drunk'.

He did not graduate from college. He moved away from his parents because he did not want their help. He received many more DUI's and was released from several places of employment. His life was deteriorating fast. He was now in his thirties and sleeping on the streets. He learned how to panhandle for money to buy beer and whiskey. He was still a very good-looking person with an infectious smile. He was well liked by all the street people so this gave him a sense of belonging. He was happy with his lifestyle on the streets.

As we looked down on this young man, we saw that he was totally wasting his time on earth. He was not a functioning entity in society. In fact, he was a parasite on society. He was not working to help others. Instead he was expecting others to help him.

Why does a soul transition to earth looking at life with blurred vision, contributing nothing to society and doing nothing to grow his soul? A life like this is a total waste for spiritual growth.

Time passed for this young man. He tried many times to stop drinking but never completed the sessions. His parents died broken hearted.

The young man was now growing old. I decided to personally try to wake him up and offer him another chance to look at his life and his soul.

I entered the local bar that he frequented and approached the old man as he swept the floors. He did this periodically for drinks.

'Hey, old man', I said, 'come over and tell me about yourself'.

He looked hesitantly at me but I told him that I would buy him lunch. He put down the broom and shuffled over.

'What do you want', he asked?

'I want to know why you have wasted your entire life by being in a drunken stupor', I said.

'It's none of your business', he said.

'Yes, it is, because I am here to personally help you get your life back on track with God before you die'.

He stared at me and then asked slowly, 'are you some type of angel or are you another goody from a church who needs points for a project or something'? I told him bluntly and very strongly that I was an angel from God. I told him that God was very DISPLEASED with his behavior because he had wasted just about his whole life.

I related to him what he had written in his life plan before he incarnated. I told him he had written that he would overcome his alcohol addiction early in his life so that he could go on to pull others out of this destructive lifestyle.

'Instead, you chose to stay in this lifestyle. You ignored all the people who tried to help you, including your parents'.

He closed his eyes and lowered his head. He was sober enough to understand everything that I had just said to him. Tears dropped onto the table. I sat patiently.

Slowly, he raised his head and asked quietly, 'are you really an angel'? I nodded my head, yes. He stared at me.

Then he asked 'who am I that God sends a special angel to'?

I told him that he is a child of God and God watches out for all of His children. I said that God was especially sad because he hadn't brought any of God's lost children back to Him.

'We angels worked very hard to wake you up. We made sure that you witnessed tragic deaths of your friends due to alcohol addiction. You saw families torn apart and children put in foster homes because one or both parents were alcoholic. Your very dear friend died in your arms from alcohol poisoning. These were the people you were supposed to save. You were to bring them back to God and help them return to their written life plan'.

'You really blew it', I said.

'This is your last chance to turn your life around. You are an old man now, but there is still time left on earth for you'.

'My advice is to kick yourself in the butt as many times as needed to get yourself clean of alcohol and get out there to bring as many souls back to God as you possibly can before your time is finished on earth'.

He closed his eyes again but I could see the tears rolling down his cheeks. When he opened his eyes, I was gone.

He sat at the table in disbelief of what had just happened. An angel actually came to him!

He asked the bartender if he saw the person he was just talking to. The bartender responded that he saw no one with the old man.

Now the old man was totally perplexed. Was this a dream, he thought? Did I pass out? Did I almost die? Was I sent back from heaven like the stories about people who die and come back after seeing a white light? I didn't see a white light, he thought, so I guess I didn't die. But there was a man here, he said to himself.

The bartender hollered to the old man asking what whiskey he wanted. These words jolted the old man as he was remembering his conversation with the angel. He immediately said 'no' and stood up and said that he was checking himself into a rehab program. The bartender laughed and said that he had heard that phrase many times before.

The old man had several setbacks in rehab but eventually he made it through the program.

This miracle was well received by us angels.

It is important to remember that miracles do not necessarily mean that a soul almost crosses over and sees great white lights.

Miracles are the turning of one's life back to God in what is perceived on earth to be impossible life situations.

Life on earth is designed to give every soul the opportunity to advance closer to God.

-Archangel Dominik

WORK ADDICTION

Spending most of your life working in a successful career or even volunteering can be both rewarding and destructive. It is rewarding when you are able to step back to evaluate your accomplishments as well as your failures.

What you do with your life on a daily basis is very important for soul development. Becoming a 'workaholic' is defined by us angels as focusing all of one's energies on the human existence. Spiritual existence is not present. Soul development is not present and therefore God is not present.

Humans are driven to this lifestyle for many reasons. The obvious is greed and the not so obvious is survival. Greed is an overwhelmingly powerful trait to succumb to. It starts small attacking a personality but grows rapidly once it becomes established. The success and monetary gratification that accompany this type of greed bring superficial happiness to that person. We say superficial happiness because that is exactly what it is. True happiness resides within the heart.

Knowing one is successful not only on the human level but also on the spiritual level removes all fear of losing material goods. By staying open to working with God, a soul can be successful not only in the material world but also in the spiritual world.

Now, the not so obvious workaholic is the person that is driven by pure survival. This is necessary for human needs but this person cannot forget spiritual needs.

Anger, many times, drives this type of person to move away from God. We angels understand the reasons for this anger, the turning away from God and the driven energy to work to keep food on the table for the family. We understand this anger but there is no reason to abandon God.

Walking away from God while on earth makes life even harder. By staying with God, we angels surround this type of workaholic and bring opportunities for advancement and monetary success to advance in life. When this soul turns away from God in anger, our help, which is God's help, is refused. This person can virtually stay in the same rut for their entire time on earth.

-Archangel Dominik

Let me tell you about two souls that I have had the privilege of showing the glory of God.

Both souls were born into families of moderate means. Their parents worked very hard for their children to succeed. Both sets of parents instilled into the young souls the importance of keeping God in their life no matter where they are or how busy they might be.

The first soul, a young man, respected his parents' hard work and always tried to do his best to succeed so they would be proud of him. He worked his way through college and even graduate school. This involved a lot of work and studying since his graduate work included medical school. He was earning good money now and enjoyed the 'good life' that his income afforded him.

He continued in the medical field specializing in cancer research. He rose higher and higher as his expertise spread throughout the medical community. Many hospitals and research centers vied to have him on their team. He liked this attention and he liked the financial rewards.

He felt driven to continually advance his research projects. He spent many hours in the research laboratory and in the hospital cancer centers. He believed he was on the verge of a great breakthrough for a rare childhood blood cancer. If he succeeded, his research could possibly apply to other types of cancer affecting children as well as adults. He wanted this success badly because he wanted the notoriety. He felt important now and liked it. He liked the money, and his position in the community and in the world.

By now, he completely neglected his wife and family. His wife had stopped asking when he would be home for dinner, or if he would attend a school event for one of their children. The children came to accept that their father was very important to the hospital and not to them. They turned to their mother for their needs.

The young doctor/researcher had moved away from God. He was very busy and felt that he was needed to save the world. He felt he did not need God in his work. He was very successful without God, so why bother.

We angels see this type of greed to be prolific in many professions. We sent many messages to his wife to help her bring his work habits under control because she desperately wanted them to have a life together again.

He was reaching the level that he believed he could truly 'cure' people of cancer once his research was complete. He couldn't let go. He never turned to us or to God to ask us to lend a hand in his research and direct him when necessary. As he moved further away from us and from God, he began to believe that he had the power to cure. He could see the world coming to him for help and advice for their cancers.

His family life was now falling apart. His wife and children moved to another city to live. He was not horribly upset with their leaving because he believed he could spend even more time with his work.

One night, as he worked late in the lab running one of the final tests of his research, a fire broke out in the building. The alarms rang throughout the building, but the young doctor ignored them, he didn't want to stop. Smoke billowed through the vents in the lab and he still didn't stop. Finally, he started coughing and choking. He staggered out into the hallway but retreated immediately. The smoke was too intense and he could feel the heat from the fire. He did not fear for his life, he feared for his research. He did not call out for us to help him. He did not call out to God. He had moved that far away from God.

The smoke overcame him quickly and he passed out. His soul moved rapidly towards us as he succumbed to the smoke and fire. We angels surrounded him and helped him orient to the ethereal world. He was not due to join us at this time of his life on earth. He made another selfish and greedy decision for the sake of fame but this time he lost.

When I met him, his transition to our world was almost complete. I told him he would be given the opportunity to return to earth. I then quickly gave him a review of his life. I showed him his successes, failures, and greed. I showed him the love that he lost when his wife and children moved away to escape his greedy work habits. I showed him how his heart had hardened when he chose to move away from God and us angels.

I told him he was being given a 'second' chance at life. It was now his decision to stay here with us in heaven or return to earth. With very saddened eyes he shook his head 'yes' that he wanted to return. He said that he feels the incredible love that is surrounding him now and would like to stay but knows that he has much to do on earth to redeem his soul and return to God as a better soul. He said that he wanted to return to God as a more advanced soul and the only way he could do that was to return to earth.

As the firemen moved throughout the smoke-filled building, they almost tripped over the doctor's body. When they put him onto the gurney before leaving for the hospital, they believed that he was dead. The doctors in the emergency room recognized their patient and worked feverishly to revive him. The nurses observed the team seemed to be working longer than usual on this patient. Everyone knew that he was dead but something was driving the doctors to continue. We angels were encouraging the doctors to stay with the patient until we were able to return his soul to his body. Once complete, the heart monitor recorded a faint beat. Our job was done and the doctors sprang into action and called in others to assist.

Recovery came quickly for the young doctor/researcher. He was anxious to return to his work. We watched him closely. His thirst for success returned. He dismissed his memory of crossing over. He talked about it in the hospital but as soon as he was strong enough to walk out, he removed the memory and the feeling of love.

His wife and children visited him while he was still in the hospital. He was very happy to see them again and his wife thought she saw a flicker of the love he once held for her and their children. But that 'flicker' died when he was released from the hospital.

The building where he did his research was destroyed along with all his research notes. He wasn't worried because he always updated his research on a flash drive. However, the flash drive was in the pocket of his lab coat the night of the fire. The lab coat was destroyed in the fire along with the flash drive. Now reality set in. Who was he without his research, he thought. He could not do any presentations without his data. He believed that no one would ask him to lecture on his outstanding work on cancer.

He believed he was a 'nobody' now.

Greed can be very cruel when it falls apart in the human psyche. Without greed, one feels helpless and lifeless with no reason to move on in life. Greed is the 'force' behind many careers.

This young doctor realized he had lost the 'force' in his life. Without this drive, he became depressed and wanted to walk away from all that had made him successful. We angels worked very hard during this time of his life. He had returned to earth to rid himself of greed and to help others through his research work. He acknowledged on the night of the fire when he passed over to us that he wanted to change and return his life to love. In order to succeed, we emphasized that he needed to remove greed from his persona and rebuild his life with God.

This is not an easy project for any human. The forces of greed are very strong on earth so this young doctor was constantly being pulled to return to his selfish life.

His wife invited him to their little girl's birthday party. She was seven years old. She was celebrating with several of her school friends. Many memories returned to the young doctor as he watched his daughter laugh and play. He remembered his childhood with his brothers and parents and how happy they were on family outings. He was remembering love.

It took several years for the doctor/researcher to duplicate and complete his research work. It was a humbling experience for him because he had many failures as he tried to replicate his work. We watched him as he grew in spiritual strength after each failed experiment. He would have success on one level, then a series of failures.

Finally, he started screaming and hollering at God for abandoning him. This was a breakthrough for us. As he shouted God's name, we filled his heart with love.

His shouting episodes slowly changed to 'help me, God'. We were elated. He was on his way, he was returning to God.

As he asked God for help with his research, thoughts, ideas and understanding flooded through his mind and he finally whispered 'thank you, God'. He completed his research and completely changed his life. God was now the 'force' in his life.

Remember, his 'miracle' was not crossing over and witnessing us angels.

His miracle was questioning WHY he was returned to earth and WHY he needed to evaluate his life.

By questioning and evaluating his near-death experience, he slowly understood that he was not on his written path in life.

His 'miracle' occurred the moment he said, 'thank you, God'.

-Archangel Dominik

Now the second soul that I had mentioned above became a workaholic out of pure need. As mentioned previously, he was well cared for in his childhood and well educated. However, as an adult he made many bad decisions with his life.

He was employed by a large manufacturing company and transferred into several departments always trying to better his career. Shortly after his last transfer, the company decided to downsize and his department was dissolved. He was given a month's salary upon exiting the company. He was not worried because he had experience from several departments within the company and believed he was very marketable.

He took some of his money and invested in the stock market, hoping for a good return in a short period of time. His stock crashed shortly after his purchase. He then decided to become self-employed and invested in a pyramid program in sales. He knew nothing about selling. He lasted about a year with that program. He then went back to school to increase his skill-set. While in school, he did not look for any type of employment to help with expenses. His monetary reserve was dwindling.

He had a wife and three children to support. They loved him dearly. It was a happy family who laughed and played together. His wife also worked but she was unable to support the family on her income.

Now the young man was becoming desperate. He needed money to care for his family. He left school and took as many jobs as possible. He was not happy with his life and how it suddenly unraveled. He started to question why God was angry with him. Why is God doing this to me, he asked himself many times?

He was growing very angry at God. He didn't deserve this kind of life, he said. He lost his house. He and his family then rented a small apartment. He worked harder and harder. During this time of working so hard and desperately, he grew away from God. We angels sent him many messages and many signs to help him secure a good job but his heart was closed. He refused to see our signs. He needed to work and now he just wanted to stay on the jobs and not go home. He wanted to run away from this spiraling crisis that he couldn't control. He didn't want to see his family because he felt that he was a failure to them and to himself.

So many good opportunities were missed by this young man because of his anger against God. He definitely needed our help to pull him out of the hole he was digging. He was working four jobs simultaneously, sleeping about four hours a night. He wouldn't let up. He never uttered one word to ask for help from us angels or from God. If he continued like this, his body would not survive and he would return to us without completing his written life plan. He was wasting his life by working so hard and long, neglecting his family and staying angry with God.

I personally sent a very strong message and sign to this young man to try to wake him up.

He recently took a position in a hospital polishing floors. He was near the emergency room when an ambulance arrived with a little girl who had been injured while riding her bicycle. She was in critical condition and he heard the emergency team announce that she was gone.

I let this young man hear most of the emergency team's conversation regarding the little girl. They unexpectedly heard a pulse beat. Excitement and chatter from the emergency room erupted…the little girl was coming back!

The young man stopped his work and stood near the emergency door in awe. He heard whispers that this was another 'miracle in the emergency room'. He saw tears in everyone's eyes when he looked through the door. When the medical staff moved out of the room, he heard them say that God was truly present. God brought the little girl back, not them, they said excitedly.

This was a lot of information for the young man to digest but it did bring God into the picture of his life. He saw that the little girl was dead and was sent back to earth. Why, he asked himself? She must have some important work to do on earth, he reasoned.

He continued on with his work at the hospital but kept on thinking and asking himself - why am I here? Working all these jobs just to survive doesn't make sense to me. He thought about the little girl often....for this little girl, there is a God, but for me there is no God.

Now this was a start for us. He was at least trying to evaluate God. With these thoughts moving through his mind, I sent a sign showing him a position in the hospital that he was highly qualified for. The position was posted on the bulletin board near his work area. As he walked by, I let the sign fall to the ground knowing he would pick it up because he had just polished the floor. As he was pinning it back onto the notification board, his eyes moved to the words 'All Applicants Welcomed'. He then read the job description, the requirements and the salary. He shook his head 'no' believing that he had been away from this type of work too long. It was exactly what he did in the large manufacturing company several years ago. But, no, he thought, this was not for him. Why should a job that he was highly qualified for suddenly present itself like this? He had previously banged on many doors for employment in his field but to no avail. No, God had walked away from him many years ago, why would He suddenly want to help him now? Without thinking, he scribbled the contact number for the position on a small piece of paper and slipped it into his pocket. He then turned to finish polishing the floors.

A week went by and we guided him to the front entrance of the hospital where the little girl was being discharged. He overheard some of the conversation with her nurse and her parents. They were discussing the little girl's miraculous recovery. He remembered the event and the thoughts that he had about God...thoughts about how God helped the little girl but had abandoned him. He stood there with tears in his eyes. He felt overwhelmed with happiness for the little girl as she passed him. He felt a peaceful, loving feeling engulf him. This feeling was us angels surrounding him with love. We were elated because he was now receiving us.

We then directed him to another bulletin board shortly after he had seen the little girl leave the hospital. Out of curiosity he scanned the board and immediately saw the position that he believed he was qualified for was still open. When he reached into his pocket for a pencil he pulled out the piece of paper with the telephone number that he recorded previously.

'What the heck, they can only say no if I apply for this job', he whispered to himself.

When he walked into the interview room, his nerves were immediately calmed. He felt a powerful, positive and happy environment within the room. He greeted his interviewers with a confidence that he had not experienced in a long time. We were there helping and guiding him through the interview.

Somehow, he knew he was being spiritually guided.

After he was hired and had settled into his new position, his wife looked at him one day and told him that it was God who directed his interview and hired him for that position. She pointed out to him all the signs that led to his interview date.

He just stared at her in disbelief and said, 'what took Him so long'?

'You', she answered.

'He was always there, but you believed you were invincible and you refused His help'.

'Tell me, what was the turning point' she asked?

'When did you start to see His signs'?

He thought carefully and the picture of the emergency room came into his mind. He then related to his wife what he overheard in the emergency room the day they admitted the injured little girl. His wife just stared at him.

Then she spoke softly and with reverence. She told him that the little girl's miracle was meant for him. It was meant for him to look deep into his heart for God. She told him the little girl came to the hospital to turn him back to God. 'You must have really moved away from God with hate in your heart for that kind of miracle to happen for you. I hope your eyes and heart are now open to God and His angels', she said.

He lowered his head and closed his eyes. Tears started streaming down his cheeks.

'I had no idea that God would go this far to reach out to help me', he said. 'I guess I really was pretty far away from Him'.

'Yes, this was truly a miracle for me', he whispered to his wife.

-Archangel Dominik

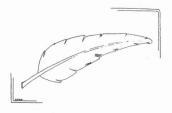

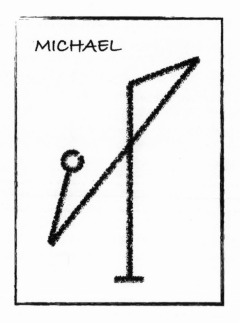

VIOLENCE

Violence between nations, within countries, and even in neighborhoods is a horrific way for humans to try to settle their differences. Tempers are always heightened, hatred abounds, and destruction is inevitable. The world is replete with negative energy.

We angels surround everyone involved in violence. We work to help them open their eyes to see and understand the hate that is associated with violence.

There are many individual 'miracles' that occur with those who are wounded by violence but *true miracles occur only when hate and anger are removed from the hearts of the injured, from the hearts of those causing injury and from the hearts of those who are caught in the crossfire.*

This has always been a big assignment for us angels because violence has existed on earth from the beginning of time. There have been many wise leaders throughout history. We surrounded and counseled them to bring peace to the people they governed. However, when the great leaders returned to us, conflicts erupted once again in their countries and the cycle of violence started over.

It is not easy to rehabilitate a human's heart that is full of hate and return it to God. We angels let small miracles occur in tumultuous areas to show that God will extend His hand into the fury of hate.

By doing miracles on a small scale, we try to bring awareness of a higher power that exists beyond violence. We inspire those involved to remember the heroic acts that they or their group performed to save innocent people caught in the middle of violence. We inspire them to get involved and relate their stories at home to help those who are away from violent conflicts understand the gravity of hatred that exists.

We work to raise awareness of senseless killing and maiming of human lives.

Let's talk about war first.

Throughout history, war has existed on every continent. In early times, as well as today, nations or groups of unsettled people have declared war for the purpose of dethroning an existing government for various reasons...land, political, religion, greed, or discontent. As these groups of unsettled people united, leaders arose and incited the troops and followers with hatred and fear of the perceived enemy.

This incitement is believed to be necessary for leaders to be successful in their battles. However, in doing so, it also sows seeds of hatred and fear.

When wars are over, individuals return to their former lives but memories of the hatred and fear that were cultivated with their fighting campaigns remain in their hearts.

Soldiers sometime talk about their battle experiences to their families and friends. Many times, the listeners receive the pervasive negative feelings of war...hate continues to grow.

It is a vicious cycle.

-Archangel Michael

Here is the story about a young man in college studying biophysics. He was very happy with his life and planned to do research in this field as soon as he received his advanced degree. However, his life changed suddenly when a bomb exploded nearby and his school buildings were severely damaged. He ran outside to see what was happening and saw several of his friends die from the attack. He couldn't see where the attack was coming from. Was it an air attack or disgruntled students who put together some hand-made bombs? He ran to his friends to see the extent of their injuries and saw they were dead. He cried holding their hands.

Who is doing this, he screamed?

Who are you?

Why do you hate us?

He could not help his friends so he ran to find safety.

The young student later found out that it was a radical group within his country. They want to conquer the world, he was told, but must be stopped now. They have already spread to many other countries destroying everything in their path. Because they have no respect for life, they kill very easily. Destruction and conquest are their ultimate goals, he quickly learned.

He talked with many friends and relatives who urged him to join the fight to stop the enemy. At first, he struggled with the thought of killing and hurting other human beings, but he remembered his school friends lying in the grass, each dead from shrapnel. He said 'yes' to himself...the enemy must be stopped. He wanted to avenge his friends' unnecessary deaths.

As he proceeded through training camps for new enlistees, hate grew in his heart. He saw picture after picture and report after report of the results of the horrific acts of these rebels. He was now ready to kill. He now had hate in his heart for the enemy. He believed he was ready to kill and perform as a dedicated soldier. He wanted to 'right' all the wrong doings of these hurtful people. He proudly accepted his first tour of duty.

Dirty trenches and extreme heat and rain, were not what the young man had in mind. He would sit in a trench for hours watching one of the enemy's strongholds. It was a very important assignment but he did not see it that way. He wanted some action. Instead, he just sat for hours at a time, watching and waiting. Little did he realize that the enemy was watching him and his fellow troops at the same time.

The enemy decided to bait the observers. They sent out some of their female and children troops for diversion. The young soldier and other military observers immediately came to attention but relaxed when they saw women and children.

Their captain alerted the troops. He knew the women and children were part of the enemy. He told his troops to hold their fire unless the women and children came within a certain range. The young man sat there and stared at the children. He could not believe they were capable of firing a weapon. They looked to be six to ten years old. Are they indoctrinated from birth to hate the world, he wondered?

The captain saw the puzzled look on the young soldier's face and told him to be prepared to fire at the children because they are the ones carrying the weapons and bombs. O MY GOD, the young man screamed to himself…IS THIS THE FACE OF WAR? How can I shoot a child, he thought? He relaxed his guard for just a second and a bullet whizzed past his head. As he looked up quickly, he saw a little boy turn around to fire again with a powerful rifle. This is insane, he thought, but images of his friends lying motionless on the grass a few months ago came vividly to his mind.

He just saw the real enemy and how they operate first hand. Now, he was ready for duty no matter the assignment.

The young man survived his trench duty and moved on to more active battles. In these battles, he could see and feel the hate that came from the enemy's camp. These negative feelings raised his determination to annihilate the enemy as best he could. He survived many horrific battles unscathed but his heart was becoming hardened by the carnage around him. He did not blink an eye or wince when he saw young children and women dying in the streets. His goal was to free the cities that were taken by the enemy, even if women and children were involved.

Members of his platoon looked to him as a hero…he seemed to have no fear. They admired him because he was cautious when necessary. He thoroughly understood and anticipated the movements of the enemy. He led many patrols and battles in this war-torn country.

He lasted five years, and the inevitable finally happened. As he and his platoon were clearing a street of the enemy, a bullet hit him in the chest. Before he hit the ground, he turned and opened fire at the target that shot him. As he hit the ground, he saw that it was a boy, about nine years old, who shot him.

The young man's body was moved quickly to a secure area while the fighting continued. The little boy's body was moved to the same area. They both lay there together, breathing but unconscious. It would be several hours before medical assistance could arrive to help them.

We angels watched closely as the bodies of both these souls struggled to stay alive. Both their souls were slowly moving closer to us. We surrounded them and encouraged them to return to earth. It was not their time to pass over to heaven.

As the two souls came closer, they recognized us and verbalized they wanted to stay. We stated, very strongly, that they were both needed on earth. We showed them the extreme hate existing in their country and how they both had this hate in their hearts on earth. We told them that they must return to earth to remove the destructive hate that exists in their hearts, and in the hearts of their families and country.

We stressed...Love must replace hate in the hearts of all mankind.

We told the young man and the little boy that it was possible for them to spread love to the world.

Now, the two souls were very close to us. They needed to return but it was their choice to stay or go. With our urging, they both decided to return. We guided them back to their bodies and assisted the medical staff with their transport to the hospital.

The young man was received into the hospital as a hero. The little boy was guarded for it was well known that this little boy shot the young man.

As they healed and became ambulatory, they both wanted to see and talk with each other knowing that they had shot one another. The first meeting was awkward and short. A few weeks passed before the two met again. This time, for reasons unknown to them, they felt drawn to each other. They felt comfortable together.

The little boy verbalized to the young man that he saw bright lights and people were talking to him shortly after he was shot. He said he didn't know who they were but they were very kind and he liked being with them. He said they showed him, on a screen, all the people dying in his town.

He looked at the young man and asked, 'why are you killing us'?

The young man just stared at the little boy. He was unable to answer his question because the little boy had just described the vision that he, himself, had when he was shot on the battlefield. He knew, at that moment, that God had spared both of them. He realized that they both returned to earth for a special task and he believed that it was not to continue being a part of the war.

The young man and little boy became very good friends after exploring their near-death experiences together and the reasons why they initially hated each other. They also researched why each had joined their fighting forces and the good and bad they had experienced in the war.

The little boy had joined his military force when he saw his parents get killed just as the young man had joined after seeing his good friends get killed. They then saw the starting point of the hatred they knew that was in their hearts.

The young man stated to the young boy that together they MUST show the world how hatred starts and how it can grow into war.

'It is difficult for me to remove my hatred for you completely', he said to the little boy, 'because I still see you with a rifle aimed at me'.

'And I have the same picture of you', the little boy answered. They both looked at each other with tears in their eyes.

The young man said quietly 'let's try'.

The young man and the little boy stayed together for many years. They first presented their stories to small groups of curious people. When the audience learned the two presenters were enemies and had shot each other, they immediately saw that a miracle had occurred for these two people. They listened intently and asked many questions because they too had much hate in their hearts for their enemies.

The news of these miracles spread slowly and steadily throughout the war-torn country. It took several years for the young man and little boy to see the effects of their 'miracle' presentations but the fighting subsided slowly as each year passed.

This miracle was intended not only for the little boy and the young man but also for everyone who listened and received into their hearts the words of the 'miracle' story.

-Archangel Michael

As I mentioned above, violence is present not only in war on a large scale, but it also occurs many times in neighborhoods on a small scale.

The young nurse had just finished her night shift at the hospital and decided to stop at a nearby restaurant to pick up a pizza. It was about nine PM when she pulled into the parking lot. As she opened the door of the restaurant, she was pushed aside by two young men rushing out. She fell to the ground and as she turned around to holler at them, she saw a gun. They had a panicked look in their eyes as she stared at them because their masks had been knocked off their faces when they bumped into her. She clearly saw their faces and they knew she could immediately identify them.

The first young man raised his gun to shoot but the other man stopped him shouting that he did not want to kill anyone in this burglary. They both decided to take her with them. The second man then shouted 'that will be kidnapping if we put her in the car'! The two robbers were clearly panicking. They didn't want to murder, kidnap or even hurt anyone. They just wanted money to buy some beer.

The first young man hollered to his friend 'drop the money and leave the nurse'.

They both ran to their car which was idling near the curb with a person in the driver's seat. It sped away as soon as they jumped in.

Several customers rushed out to help the nurse. The police and ambulance arrived shortly and transported the young nurse to the hospital where she worked.

There was chaos in the restaurant as the police interviewed customers and staff for information about the robbers. No one could identify the young boys because they were well covered from their head to their shoes. They said the men did not talk. They gave a note to the worker behind the register demanding money.

The owners were furious because this was the second time in two months that they were robbed. They had talked about getting a gun for protection and this robbery made the decision for them…they decided to buy a gun the next day. Their anger was growing.

The young nurse was released from the hospital the next day with cuts and bruises. She strongly feared that the young boys might look for her because she could identify them. She gave detailed descriptions to the police of the two men as well as a description of their car.

She stayed away from the restaurant for several weeks fearing the robbers would be looking for her. As the weeks passed, her fear turned to anger. She was angry because she felt her every move was being watched. She was angry because she felt unsafe wherever she went. She was angry because she knew she was a target for violence.

The young men were very fearful that night as they sped away. They were just out to have a good time. They needed extra money to buy some beer. They didn't think it was a big deal to try to rob a small restaurant. They were smart enough to camouflage themselves and unfortunately one of the young men had his father's handgun. They were all innately good but could easily be led in the wrong direction.

They decided to 'lay low' for a couple of weeks hoping the police/detectives would put this case on the back burner so more important cases could be investigated. However, they continued to worry about the young nurse whom they knocked down as they ran from the restaurant.

The restaurant owners purchased a gun. With this weapon in their possession, their anger increased. They did not like living in fear especially when their restaurant was located in a very low crime area. They became alert and alarmed whenever young men would come into the restaurant. They hesitated to serve them.

The young nurse returned to the restaurant after being absent for several weeks. They were happy to see her and talked to her about the robbery. When she described the young men's faces, they became fearful because two young men having similar characteristics were in the restaurant about two nights ago. This made them angry because they thought they were getting good at reading their customers for potential problems. The young nurse told the restaurant owners not to worry. She believed they would not come back here because their facial descriptions were given to the police. However, she did express her own fears and anger and that she, too, had purchased a gun.

We angels were now watching the rise of fear and anger in all who had been affected by this robbery. Their fear was turning directly to anger. Now that guns were in the picture, violence could erupt easily.

Two young men entered the restaurant that evening and sat at a nearby table as the young nurse sipped her wine. She recognized them as quickly as they recognized her. She slipped her hand into her purse for her gun. The owners reached for their gun when they saw the young girl's facial expression when she looked at the young men who had just entered the restaurant. The young men felt panic and reached for their gun also.

Violence was imminent.

The young men wanted to remove the young nurse who could identify them. The young nurse feared for her life and the restaurant owners feared for themselves and the young girl. Anger was rising in the restaurant as the young men walked toward her table. The owners hesitated behind the counter but their gun was ready to fire.

The door of the restaurant opened and two policemen walked in. They had been watching the restaurant since the robbery. They approached the owners and asked if all was okay. The owners nodded yes, nervously. The police could see their gun and sensed something was wrong. As they turned around to leave, one of the young men grabbed the young girl and waved his gun.

Violence was erupting.

A lone gentleman sat nearby observing. He immediately stood up when the young man grabbed the nurse. He walked slowly toward them. His voice was very strong and echoed throughout the restaurant. He demanded the nurse be released. The young men laughed and pointed the gun at him. The police now had their guns drawn and pointed at the young men. A large white light suddenly beamed in through the window behind the tall gentleman and blinded the young men. As they protected their eyes, their gun dropped to the floor. The gentleman picked it up. He also demanded that the nurse and the owners put their guns away. He then handed the young men to the police. Before he left, he stated very strongly to everyone in the restaurant...

VIOLENCE DOES NOT BEGET VIOLENCE REMOVE YOUR ANGER TO MAKE THIS A SAFE PLACE TO GATHER.

As the police removed the young men, they asked if anyone knew the man who had just averted a very violent scene. Everyone looked around to thank the gentleman but the brave man was not there. No one saw him enter and no one saw him leave. But he was real, they insisted.

Yes, he was real because he was one of us angels.

Was this a 'miracle'? Yes, this truly was a miracle because several lives were spared and anger was dispersed in the lives of all those involved. The young nurse looked at her gun sitting on the table and immediately disarmed it saying she was not a violent person. The restaurant owners looked at her and said that they too did not want to be a part of violence. They disarmed their gun also.

The three discussed how their feelings of fear had led them to anger and how anger took them to potential violence. They talked about how they could keep their fear and anger under control and how they could use these feelings to be prepared but not violent. They all felt relieved and happy not only to be alive but also to have taken the steps to remove violence from their lives.

They believed the tall gentleman who interceded in the event was truly from God.

They talked about this gentleman, the blinding light and the fearful event in the restaurant to all who would listen to their story.

-Archangel Michael

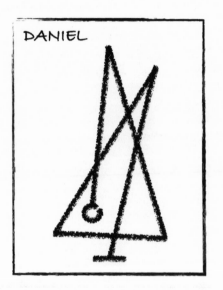

ABUSE

Abuse is a very strong word and a very strong act that occurs on earth.

We angels and archangels are always on alert to monitor this type of horrendous treatment. Abuse can be both mental and physical. It is very damaging not only to the injured but also to the offender.

How can this be, you might say?

How can an abuser be damaged when **they** inflict pain on another?

Usually, the offender himself is already damaged or hurting internally and wants to transfer their pain onto another. Sometimes this can become a vicious cycle in families.

Our role as guardians and protectors is to help the abused person move out and away from their perpetrator. We then direct the abused person to report abusive behavior to the proper authorities, and to get both physical and mental help. This is very important because once the abused person begins to heal many scars start to form. Anger and hatred can grow from these scars...the abused person can then become an abuser fighting the ghosts of their abusive past. This is how the cycle begins and continues.

Both types of abuse, physical and mental, include all walks of life...children as well as adults. Mental abuse can be more subtle than physical abuse. It may take a longer period of time to be recognized.

Getting away from mental abuse can be very difficult because the abused soul *must* remove themselves from the abuser. If the abused soul is young, the family may not relinquish the child except under court order. If the abused soul is married or living with another and is not able to afford to live on their own income, the abused soul, reluctantly, will stay to continue its lifestyle. If the abuser is an employer, the abused employee will stay in their position for as long as possible, fearful of not finding another position of comparable income or fearful of a hurtful reference that could affect their career.

Yes, these scenarios and many more exist to propagate and extend abuse.

-Archangel Daniel

The young man had been working for a local manufacturing company for about six years when his boss retired. The new boss was recruited from outside the company and had several years of experience in the manufacturing area where the young man worked. The new boss was friendly to all the employees and worked to know them on a personal level. The young man was pleased with this new boss and was looking forward to working with him in order to get promoted and move up in the manufacturing business.

After a few months, the new boss seemed to change. His personality would swing from happy and lighthearted to angry and nasty. He seemed to single out a few employees for public reprimands and ridicule. The young man was one of these selected employees. He would stand erect and strong when the verbal whiplashing was directed at him. He took in every hurtful word that was hurled at him. He wanted to learn the manufacturing business so badly that he believed that these verbal abuses would strengthen and educate him. He did not see this behavior as abusive.

The young man learned to stay in this environment because he grew up with similar abuse from both his parents. They scolded him for everything including good grades on his report cards…they wanted him to do better. He learned how to exist in this negative environment and grew up believing he was not intelligent enough to go to college or perform well in anything he did. So, he stopped trying because he did not want to be 'put down' by his parents and his siblings. He was very proud the day he announced his new job to his family. They immediately laughed and ridiculed him. He gradually withdrew from his family even though he needed to live with them. However, he never hated his parents or siblings for their abusive behavior toward him.

The young man decided to apply for a new position within the company. He had been there for eight years now and felt very confident in the work that he did and how the manufacturing process operated in his department. He wanted to move to another department to learn another aspect of manufacturing. His boss ridiculed him for thinking that he was capable of moving on. His boss had always given the young man marginal reviews but the young man did not think badly of this. It reminded him of his parents and how they treated him when he showed them his school report card. He took the ridicule from his boss as a 'push' to make him work harder.

He fellow workers, in the meantime, had filed a grievance complaint against the new boss. They asked him to sign this grievance with them but he refused. Again, he remembered his parents' actions and was afraid of retaliation. His friends could not convince him that he was being abused. He truly believed this type of treatment was part of the learning process of life. He told his friends that he was applying for a new position in another department and would be moving away from this boss. He told them that he would be okay.

When the young man's friends found out that he was denied the new position due to a lack of competence, they were furious. They knew immediately that their boss was the cause of this denial. They all went, as a group, to the personnel department to address this denial. The personnel officer was very interested in what the group related about their young friend and also about their boss and the interactions in the department. The group presented the personnel officer with the grievance they had written and signed and explained why their friend's name was not with the other signatures. Personnel received all this information and assured the group of workers that they would be contacted for more information when needed. The group did not feel they were successful with their efforts to bring awareness of the abusiveness that existed in their department.

A few weeks later, the young man jumped with joy when he received a phone call from the other department. He announced to all his friends that he had just gotten the new position. They jumped with joy with him. Their boss walked in to see them all slapping backs and hollering congratulations to their co-worker. They all froze the moment they saw him.

He ordered the group to return to their stations immediately. He was extremely furious over the news and the young man's promotion. The young man sheepishly came to the boss and said 'thank you for all your help. I got the new position'.

The boss looked the young man straight in the eyes and said, 'you will pay for this'.

He suddenly threw open his arm and grabbed a metal bar that was next to a machine and lunged at the young man. The young man, stunned, stepped to one side and the boss tumbled into a machine that was running. The whole department stopped and stared in disbelief for a few seconds. The young man ran to turn off the power to the machine.

We angels were always in this department working to protect and direct the employees away from this abusive boss. Most of the employees received our messages to file the grievance against their boss in an effort to stop his harmful actions.

The abusive boss was abused himself physically and mentally as a child not only by his parents but also by some teachers in grade and high school. He learned how to survive in this type of environment but he never let go of it. He made it a part of his persona in dealing with other people and grew to thrive on hurting not only his family members but also everyone who came under him in the chain of employment positions.

Through the years many complaints were filed against him at different places of employment but he was always able to wiggle his way out of the accusations. When he felt the pressure from his employers to change his behavior or if he was placed on probation, he simply changed positions or moved to a new company. He felt very secure with his life. He was proud of his abusive nature and the fact that he was able to bully employees to increase their workload in order to secure higher bonuses for himself.

This abusive boss crossed over to us following his fall into the machine as a result of lunging at the young man with a metal bar in an effort to beat him. The young man shut the machine down but not in enough time to prevent injury. The paramedics arrived to transport the injured boss to the hospital. The emergency crew in the hospital worked diligently to keep this injured man alive. His body was very badly broken with bone and organ injuries. Even though they lost his heartbeat several times, they would not give up.

We angels received the soul of this injured man but before he completely moved to our side, we encouraged him to return to earth. We showed him exactly what had happened to cause his death including his abusive move to cause injury to the young man. He said that move was in self-defense. We reminded him that he was not on earth. He could not try to change the truth with us. We then showed him his exact moves with the metal bar and we allowed him to hear his abusive accusations to the young man. He was stunned. He had no way out.

We then reminded him that he had experienced abusiveness as a child but he was supposed to learn from that type of treatment, not make it a part of his life. His written goal was to recognize abusiveness in others and work to stop it. He had also written in his life plan that he would create an organization dedicated to erasing abusiveness.

He watched with tears in his eyes as we showed him his own abusive actions. We reminded him that it was his choice to return to earth or stay with us. By returning, he would be able to change his behavior and raise awareness to the prevalence of abusiveness.

As the doctors removed their masks and gloves and declared the injured man dead, the heart monitor sounded loud and clear that his heart was beating again. The emergency crew jumped into action with smiles on their faces. One of the doctors exclaimed that they were all witnessing a true miracle. The doctor said that he hoped this person remembers his time on the other side. He told the other doctors that when a soul returns, as this one just did, it is usually for a very special reason.

The injured boss recovered slowly. He had many hours to review his life. The young man was elated that his former abusive boss survived. His co-workers were astonished that he felt this way. They told him that anyone as nasty as this boss deserved to die. By living, they stated, he would continue to abuse and hurt others. They believed death was the best way for this type of behavior to end. The young man, who received the brunt of this abusive behavior, felt differently. He told his friends at work that he believed their boss would change because God was giving him a second chance at life. They all just stared at him with disbelief.

The young man visited his abusive boss many times in the hospital. His boss was initially very angry because of his injuries and the long road to recovery.

He continued to abuse the young man during the hospital visits until one day the young man looked his abusive boss in the eyes and asked, 'why did God let you return to earth?'

He continued, 'did you see and talk to anyone when you crossed over'?

His boss screamed at him stating '**what does that have to do with me surviving the accident that YOU caused**'?

The young man was stunned and very hurt. Just then a doctor walked in and asked what the commotion was all about. The young man remained quiet while his boss continued to say that the young man caused his accident and that he was very angry at what the young man had done to him. The doctor stood firmly next to the bed, looked the man in his eyes and stated strongly that the young man saved his life. He told him that he should be very thankful and not angry.

The doctor then lowered his voice and reminded the abusive boss of his meeting with the angels when he crossed over to heaven. He asked the man to remember his abusive behavior review with the angels. The man in the bed denied any encounters with the angels.

The doctor looked directly into the abusive man's eyes and whispered strongly to him...

'You tried to change the truth on the other side and you are changing the truth again! Remember your reason for returning to earth and start changing your behavior now. The young man that you abused for several years was directed to you to help you change your behavior. You refused to change no matter how hard the young man tried to help you'.

The doctor then turned and walked out of the room. The young man was in awe of what he just witnessed. He quietly said to his boss that the doctor was a messenger from God. The young man quickly left the hospital room.

As the abusive boss healed physically, he let the young man into his life. He asked for detailed descriptions of his abusiveness. The young man helped his boss slowly see his hurtful actions and together they traveled through life identifying physical and mental abusive behavior. Together they worked to raise awareness about the prevalence of abusiveness not only in the work environment but also with children in the family environment, with parents, and with high school and college students. It was a small start that grew steadily and spread locally, nationally and eventually to many other countries

Our intersession was necessary for this behavior to be addressed on earth. Two miracles were needed. The important part of this miracle was that the abusive boss remembered his encounter with us even though he tried to deny it. He immediately slipped back into his abusive behavior as he healed. Another miracle was then needed to open his mind and heart to accept that he was given a second chance to continue living his life.

As you read this second chance experience, look at your own life.

What path are you walking now?

Are you living a selfish, or jealous, or abusive life?

Are you walking with your mind and heart open to see the love that surrounds you?

Do you understand and help those who may cross your path who are sad or lonely?

Welcome us angels into your life every day to help guide you through your life choices.

Be aware...many miracles will be coming your way when you walk with us.

-Archangel Daniel

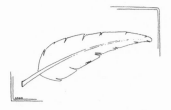

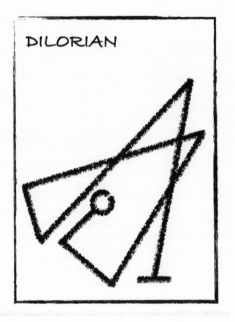

DILORIAN

HOMELESSNESS

Homeless people receive a large number of experiences and miracles. They recognize miracles among themselves but as they stay in this state of living day-to-day, they communicate these 'miracles' only to the homeless who surround them.

There are also homeless people who have been able to rise out of this lifestyle and return to society.

You may wonder why some remain in this state of living and why others are able to move out of it.

If there are 'miracles' with homeless people, why are the majority left behind?

Homeless people have existed on earth for thousands of years. Some people are born into homelessness, some are born into poverty and slowly slip in homelessness and some choose to be homeless.

We angels always surround these homeless beings. We work to show them how to improve their lives, build their confidence and try to direct them out of their state of homelessness. When they open their hearts to us in desperation, they receive our signs and messages and that is when the 'miracle' begins.

Miracles are truly needed with this group on earth because they have lost touch with their souls and the reasons they have incarnated to earth. Many have virtually given up and have accepted this way of life.

The homeless, who have chosen this state following a successful childhood, have also given up on their life on earth.

Because of the tremendous feeling of helplessness among this group of people, many angels walk freely among these people showering them with God's love.

- Archangel Dilorian

Let me first tell you about a middle-aged woman who walked away from a very successful business that she had started. It was her passion. She dreamed of owning her own business when she was a teenager. She worked for a clothing store during high school and college moving through many positions. When she graduated college with a business degree, she was promoted to assistant manager. She was happy because she was able to use the marketing skills she had acquired in college to help increase sales for this store.

Life was good for this young girl. Her talents in business were recognized as she was promoted to the corporate office. She worked very long and hard in this position forgoing a social life with friends and family. She continued at this frantic pace for about ten years when she finally listened to the constant chatter of her friends who kept urging her to open her own business. They insisted that if she had to work hard and long hours, she should do it for herself. Through their encouragement, she left her high-powered job and opened the doors to her own specialty boutique.

The shop was an immediate success. It was located in a premier shopping area and expertly designed. The young woman worked long hours at the shop and more hours after closing tending to the finances, advertising, special orders and inventory. She was happy through all this hard work. Her shop was her dream come true.

Her friends were very happy for her and encouraged her to join them periodically for dinner or a drink after work. She always declined feeling the pressure to stay ahead of the day-to-day operations. Slowly and steadily, her friends drifted away. She didn't notice at first, but after a few years at this grueling pace, she suddenly felt lonely. She called a couple of her friends. They were surprised to hear from her but they had moved on with their lives and were not free to join her for dinner. She was surprised and felt hurt not realizing that she did the same to them for several years. She kept reaching out to friends, acquaintances, and even frequent customers. No one was available to socialize with her. She shrugged this off and buried herself deeper into the demands of her shop.

She had been in business successfully for about ten years when her sales started to show a decline. She believed it was due to a slower economy and believed that she had enough reserve to survive if she carefully watched her inventory. She didn't take notice that several large discount stores recently opened nearby. Foot traffic into the shop declined steadily for several months. She learned of the discount stores from a customer and decided to investigate for herself. She saw many of the same items that she carried in her shop. She could not sell them for the lower prices.

The middle-aged woman closed the doors to her shop with tears in her eyes. This was her 'life' she said to herself. This was her 'child'. It is no more. She stayed in her house for several weeks mourning the loss of her business, her child. She had no one to console her. She didn't have the energy or desire to start a new business or even to seek outside employment. She wallowed in her sorrow.

Two of her friends always volunteered during the holidays at a nearby 'soup kitchen'. They noticed a new face in line and smiled to welcome her. They stopped smiling as they recognized the middle-aged woman as their friend who previously owned the boutique. They both said hello to their friend but she just smiled and kept moving along. She did not recognize them. They hardly recognized her. She was disheveled and unkempt. This was not like her, the friends remarked to each other. Their friend was always stylishly dressed. What happened, they said? When they had finished working the 'soup' line, they looked around to talk with her, but she had left. They felt they needed to find her and help her.

They searched for several days and found their friend living on the street surrounded by her belongings, which included a blanket and some food. They were shocked and a little hesitant to approach. They roused her from her sleep to start a conversation. The woman was frightened and recoiled. They explained that they were her friends from when she was in college. They asked about her boutique. Tears rolled down her cheeks. She lost it, she said, due to competition and did not want to talk about it. She asked them to go away.

We angels watched very closely the mental state of this homeless woman. There was no reason for her to be homeless. She was a well-educated and successful businessperson. She had a setback in the business world but this was a challenge given to her to advance her life. She needed to pick herself up and move on. There was nothing for her to gain by dropping out of society, dropping out of life. We must get her back on her life's plan soon. She was getting too comfortable being homeless.

She continued homeless for several years. She stayed in the same area of the city and made many friends who were also homeless. They taught her survival techniques for bad weather and how to improve her begging style. In the meantime, her health was deteriorating. She had a constant cold and was always coughing. Her homeless friends advised her to go to a nearby hospital. They assured her that she would be well taken care of. These words jarred a memory of her college life. While in college, she went to the hospital with pneumonia and the doctors warned her to always be careful when she got respiratory infections. Instinctively, she knew that she had pneumonia but did not want to receive medical help.

Her condition deteriorated as she laid in her cardboard house on the street. Her homeless friends just passed her by believing that she needed the rest to recover. A policeman who routinely patrolled that area watched the motionless woman with concern. He tried to rouse her several times to make sure that she was still alive. Finally, he called an ambulance. He saw her labored and shallow breathing and knew her health was failing. He followed her to the hospital and waited outside the emergency room giving details to the hospital personnel. Within an hour, the medical staff opened the door to say that she had stopped breathing. As they were giving details at the desk, the policeman noticed a man slip into the room with the homeless woman. He thought the man was from the hospital morgue. The man emerged from the emergency room and walked directly to the medical staff. He told them to return to the room because the patient was recovering. They rushed in to see the patient breathing and color returning to her body. Without questioning, they immediately went to work to help the homeless woman return to life. The policeman stayed a while longer wondering about the identity of the man who slipped into the emergency room.

As the homeless woman moved closer to us angels, she reached out for us to help her cross over to this side. We gently encouraged her to return to earth because her life was not yet finished there. We told her that she was wasting precious time on earth by dropping out of life as she did. She said that she was tired and wanted to come 'home'. She said that she believed that she was a failure in life because her business failed. She felt that her peers would judge her as an incompetent businessperson. She just wanted to run and hide from the world. Please, she begged, bring me over to your side. Very strongly, we reiterated that she had a lot more work to do on earth. We told her that we would guide and help her but she needed to return to earth and change. She needed to open her heart and her mind to receive our help. She hesitated her forward movement towards us. She then nodded and whispered 'yes' I will return.

The moment that she agreed to return to earth, Archangel Tonurret walked into the emergency room to help her soul reunite with her body. He massaged her heart until it was able to pump on its own. When her organs began receiving blood from her now beating heart, Archangel Tonurret left the room.

When the doctors and nurses completed the recovery tasks, they stood and looked at each other in silence. They had just witnessed a powerful miracle and they knew it. One nurse had tears in her eyes.

Another said that he would never look at a homeless person as worthless any more. He stated...*this has taught me that every soul on earth is here for a reason and I am not the one to judge their life. God returned this homeless lady to earth and I am happy that I was chosen to witness this miracle.* Everyone agreed and they were all thankful to have witnessed her return to earth.

When the policeman heard the full story from the medical staff, he too realized that he was chosen to be a part of this great miracle. He felt guilty that he let the woman lay on the street in her makeshift home for several days before he decided to help her. He resolved that he would never do that again.

Following her recovery in the hospital, the homeless woman returned to retrieve her belongings on the street. She looked around her and saw her homeless friends staring at her. They saw that she had changed. She smiled and greeted them happily. They were fearful at first but gradually warmed up to her. She told them her story of talking to the angels and returning to her body. She said that she was told that she still had a lot of work to do on earth and she was ready to start now. She told her friends that she wanted to help them. As they surrounded her, they felt an abundance of love emanating from her presence.

This 'miracle' was intended not only for the homeless woman but also for the hospital medical staff, the policeman and her homeless friends.

The woman's eyes were opened to see the reason why she incarnated to earth.

The hospital staff was given the opportunity to witness this 'miracle' so that they might look at their own lives, their own purpose in life and their prejudices of the patients who cross their path in the medical environment.

The 'miracle' woke the policeman to his complacent attitude toward homeless people. He opened his eyes to see that a homeless person is just like him trying to survive life on earth. He came to understand that the homeless had lost their drive to experience life as it was written before they incarnated to earth.

The homeless friends of the woman slowly opened their eyes to understand that they are also on earth for more important reasons than living on the city streets and begging for food and money.

Yes, this was a true 'miracle' intended for more than one person.

Be aware when you hear of the events of a 'miracle' and remark how lucky a person was to be returned to earth to complete their life. Look at your life and evaluate where you are with your soul development process.

The 'miracle' you are hearing about may have been intended for you also.

- Archangel Dilorian

Homelessness is pervasive. It is everywhere...in all countries, large and small cities, and even remote areas of the world.

A young man was born into homelessness. His mother lived on the streets in a very large city when he was born. She did not go to a hospital for fear of losing her baby to the authorities. With the help of her street friends, she was able to care for her baby. She did not think of what was best for him at the time because she felt comfort holding her baby and giving him her love. She was lonely and unhappy. She was able to hide the infant from the authorities for several years. As a toddler, the little boy was happy on the streets with his mother's friends. Many of her friends were educated and lovingly played and worked with him to develop his motor and speech skills. He never cried for attention or from hunger. Everyone took care of him.

When he was old enough for school, his mother registered him in a nearby public school. She was well-educated herself and knew education was necessary for him to move out of this homeless environment if he wanted.

She remembered her corporate life vividly and vowed never to return to that lifestyle. She was very happy living on the streets away from the frantic competitive life that she lived several years ago.

As the boy grew older, he recognized that he was different. Many of his school friends asked him over to their house. He liked how they lived and how much they had to eat. They asked many times where he lived and he would answer with a very vague address. By middle school, he was torn between wanting the lifestyle of his friends and the lifestyle on the streets surrounded by his mother and her friends.

He learned how to survive on the streets. He learned how to beg as well as how to steal. His mother saw this behavior but still refused to return to society and use her educational skills to protect her son from possible illegal behavior. The son loved his mother but knew nothing of her past. He believed she had always lived on the streets.

The young boy completed his high school education at the insistence of his mother. However, he did not want to continue his education. He liked his life on the streets. He was free. During his high school years, his mother constantly showed him the bad effects of drugs by pointing to people asleep next to buildings telling him that they were passed out from drugs. She also brought his attention to authorities making drug raids nearby. She taught him that using drugs was a dead-end life style but homelessness was another lifestyle and honorable in its own way. As he grew older and saw more of life, he could not understand his mother's statements on homelessness.

He continued on with this lifestyle for several years after completing high school. He made friends with a lot of people who lived on the street and helped whenever someone needed his assistance. He was friendly with many of the police and social workers who patrolled his neighborhood. They would always ask him why he was homeless. He told them he was 'born' into homelessness and had never slept in a bed or in a house. They wanted to help him but he always said 'no'. My life is here, he would say, these people need me.

The social workers saw true love in his eyes when he talked about his homeless friends. They wanted him to join their team believing he would be a true asset because he lived the homeless life and cared about the people on the street. He declined many times. He said he didn't want to leave them to go to college. I would be away from them too long, he would say.

One day, he met one of his high school friends near the school. The friend recognized him and asked him to lunch. The young man accepted because he was hungry. The friend noticed his disheveled clothing and asked what he was doing in life. The young man just answered that he was helping a lot of homeless people. The friend was happy to hear what sounded like a productive life but couldn't understand why he looked so shabby.

The friend boasted that he recently completed college and was joining an international organization. He explained that he would be going to a foreign country for about a year or so to help underprivileged people. The young man stared at him in disbelief asking him why he needed to leave the country to help people? Look around you, the young man said, look at all the people who live on the streets right here. They have no home, no food, and no bed.

The friend responded he believed that these people chose to live on the street, they chose the homeless lifestyle. 'They don't need my help', he said. 'They need to wake up and help themselves'.

'How do you know that', the young man asked? 'How do you know that all homeless people, children included, choose poverty and homelessness'?

They stared at each other, and then the young man said quietly to his friend that he was born into homelessness. He stated that he did not 'choose' this lifestyle.

The young man then asked his friend if he knew where the 'underprivileged' people that he wanted to help in foreign countries lived. 'Do you think that they have small apartments with beds and blankets to keep them warm'?

'No', the young man said, 'they live on the streets in the very poor sections of their towns and cities. They live just like these homeless people here in this section of town. The underprivileged people that you want to help are hungry, disheveled and looking for love and a helping hand just like these people are'.

His friend responded that he wanted to help underprivileged people become productive citizens in their country. 'I want to help them by nourishing and educating them. That is what they want', he said, staring at the young man.

The young friend said that he felt that many homeless people that he witnessed in his area were lazy and did not want to better their life.

'How can you say that', the young man asked?

'Look at me. I graduated high school and I am still here. I know how to exist to help these people. Through social workers, that I have come to know, I have been able to direct more than two handfuls of people to move from homelessness to becoming productive citizens'.

'How is my life, working with homeless people, different from the life that you will have working with underprivileged people? I am interpreting that you associate homeless people as street people under the common word of bum', the young man stated.

'And, I believe, you associate underprivileged people as people who do not live on streets, who are just very poor and lack in opportunity to advance to a better lifestyle'.

The young man's friend nodded his head yes.

'I am so sorry that you see life that way', the young man said. 'All people are equal no matter their status in life. Just because you view a person as a 'bum' does not mean that person is worthless and not worthy of receiving a helping hand. Remember my words, the young man said, and come find me when you return from your goodwill trip. People need help wherever you travel, wherever you live, from here to all areas of the world. That is just how life is on earth'.

At the request of several social workers, the young man expanded his work with homeless people to other areas of his city. He was very good with helping those who had become angry and bitter with their homeless state. He was able to help them open their minds to see and acknowledge their present status in life. He showed them that by accepting their misfortune they could then start rebuilding their lives. He led the way to their recovery. He gave them an abundance of love and constantly repeated to them to trust not only him but to trust God also.

The young man was an 'angel' to many homeless people. In fact, he was affectionately called the 'street angel'.

One day, he entered a new section of town and as he walked among the 'homeless' he suddenly recognized his high school friend who had gone to a foreign country to help underprivileged people a few years ago. When he started to talk to his friend, he realized his friend was totally overwhelmed with life. The young man took his friend to a nearby coffee shop. The friend told him that when he arrived in the designated country, he was very enthusiastic to help as many people as he could. He said he gave and gave and the more he gave the more they took but he could not see any progress. I wanted to raise them up out of their poverty so they could lead a productive life just as I do, he said. I tried so hard. I even went to several other countries, believing it would be different and I could witness how successful I was at helping people. It kept getting worse, he said.

'How did you view the people you wanted to help', the young man asked his friend?

'I saw them as less fortunate than I but hesitant to take my handouts. I believed them to be less intelligent than I so I didn't try teaching them how to help themselves. After seeing all this, I believed them to be a lower class of human beings. I stayed two years…I thought that was enough. I did my duty for humankind', he uttered with some sarcasm.

'Why are you living on the streets now', the young man asked?

'I'm tired of society; I'm tired of the rat race that's out there. I came back and got a job in a hospital as a social worker. They liked me because of my experience overseas. But it's all the same, he said. I can't see how I am helping people. I don't see any results. All these people are worthless'.

The young man responded by reminding his friend that he was now living among those whom he perceived as 'worthless' and 'bums'.

The young man continued to check in on his friend, trying to make sense of his outlook on life. He could not understand how he could dislike homeless and underprivileged people yet become homeless himself.

The young man visited his friend often trying to see how he could help him. His attitude seemed to get worse with each visit. The young man could see that depression was entering his friend's psyche. He was worried because he knew that with depression comes self-doubt and low self-esteem. All this leads to suicidal thoughts. He saw it often.

As the health of his friend deteriorated, the young man tried to get him to go to a hospital but his friend declined. One morning the young man found his friend unconscious and immediately called an ambulance. His friend was unconscious for several days. The doctors said he was suffering from severe malnutrition, dehydration and pneumonia.

When he opened his eyes, he saw an elderly gentleman sitting next to his bed. He thought it was a doctor, and then he thought it was his father but his father had died several years ago. He closed his eyes hoping this person would go away. When he opened his eyes again, the person was still there.

'Who are you', he asked?

'Why are you here'?

The gentleman spoke very softly but sternly. 'What are you doing with your life', the gentleman asked?

'Why are you wasting it'?

'You were given all the tools and the opportunities to fulfill your written goals and now you are just walking away from what you had planned to accomplish while on earth'.

'You know you are about to die and return to heaven. I can't stop it if this is what you choose'.

'Think about what I am about to say and make your choice. Not many people get a second chance like this'.

'Your goal on earth was to remove your prejudices. You wanted to remove your haughty attitude. You always felt you were above most others. You believed you were better than everyone. You prepared well for this assignment but now you have given up. If you stay on earth, remember these words...*no one is any better than anyone else no matter the circumstances that each may be experiencing on earth. We sent you your high school friend, who lived a homeless life, to help pave the way for you... USE HIM*'.

The young man stopped by the hospital to see how his friend was doing. When he entered the intensive care unit, he saw a flurry of activity around his friend. He later learned that the instruments showed that his friend had stopped breathing and just as they were ready to remove his body, a blip sounded from the monitor indicating that he was not completely gone. He recovered slowly at first but progressed steadily showing that his body would make a full recovery.

He related his experience of the elderly gentleman to the young man who just smiled at him when he heard the story. The young man told him that he was being given a second chance at life and that he should evaluate why he returned and use his time wisely before he exists earth for good.

The young man told his friend in the ICU that the elderly gentleman that he saw sitting next to his bed giving him words of advice about his life was not an ordinary person who stopped by to visit. The young man continued to say that the elderly gentleman was a messenger from God. I believe it was an angel talking to you because you were very close to crossing over to the other side. His friend looked at him in disbelief because he had no idea that he had died and returned to earth.

The young man stared at his bedridden friend. He extended his hand and said that he didn't know why he was given a second chance at life but he would be very happy to stand by him and help him return to his written path in life.

A miracle was needed here to show the young friend how far away he had gotten from his goals on earth. He literally gave up on his path in life, which would have led him to successfully achieve the reason that he incarnated to earth.

The young homeless man recognized the miracle that had just occurred and knew his friend was surrounded by powerful angels to push him back to earth. He believed that if his friend had angels helping and surrounding him, then the miracle had some meaning for him also.

The miracle was intended for both of them.

The young, homeless man then closed his eyes and whispered *'thank you, God, for allowing me to be a part of your work'.*

-Archangel Dilorian

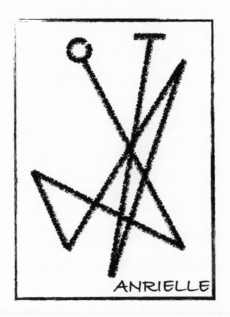

SILENT MIRACLES

Silent miracles are 'miracles' that happen every day. They are not recognized on earth as 'miracles' with the presence of angels and God. They are usually interpreted as a 'change in lifestyle' or a 'waking up to life' or even 'finally growing up'.

These changes that you see occurring regularly in life are due to us angels working to get individuals back on their written path as soon as we see them wandering away. We work to keep all individuals as close to their heavenly plan as possible. The further away one travels from their plan, the more difficult and even dangerous life may become for them.

That is why we need to stay close to all humans as they walk through life...to keep them from destroying not only themselves but also others. If they get to the point where they return to us and their written plan is not complete, they have a small window of opportunity to return to earth. We receive that soul and encourage it to return but the soul may choose to stay with us. That is their right…it is called free will. That soul will then be received back into heaven to rest.

The soul will review its life on earth with the angels to learn and understand how it moved away from its written plan. We angels then start preparing that spirit for another transition to earth to complete the previous life plan.

So, you can see why these 'silent miracles' are so important. The more individuals respond to our help, the greater chance they have to succeed in completing their 'reason' to be on earth and thus to further develop their soul.

Here are a few examples to help you recognize 'silent miracles' as true 'miracles'.

When you recognize a positive change in a friend or relative, know angels are present helping to redirect that person's life to get them back on track with God.

Do not judge the other person, but look at your own life…are you on your own 'set' track with God?

Only you can answer that.

-Archangel Anrielle

The beautiful young girl had just completed college and was gainfully employed in her field of study, fashion design. She grew up in a happy household with very loving parents and two brothers. Everyone was very proud of her because she was living her dream. As a child she would sit for hours drawing wedding gowns, ballroom dresses, summer and winter attire. She would sit for hours sketching her own designs.

Now that she was in the workforce, she believed she was headed for greatness. She was competitive and always kept her eyes open to grab a new account in the hopes that it would bring her fame and fortune.

She observed her co-workers and could not understand why they were so complacent in their positions as fashion designers. She asked them why they didn't seem excited with their work. Most responded that they were very excited and happy with their work but they had learned how to pace themselves with the demands of the job. They told her that if she kept going at her speed she would burn out in a few years. She asked if they wanted to be recognized and be famous for their work? They said that they were already recognized and that they were happy and pleased with the work they produced. The company, they stated, liked their work and they saw their names in many department stores. That wasn't good enough for her. She wanted to be the next Oscar de la Renta or Ralph

Lauren of the world. Her friends told her that recognition comes ONLY with time and perseverance.

On her own time, the young girl traveled to many fashion shows introducing herself to the celebrities in the fashion world who attended. She believed she was advancing her career by mentioning these names to her coworkers and to her bosses when she returned from her travels. They kept telling her to slow down, to enjoy her life and improve her design skills. She was told that her designs were very good and creative but she needed experience to bring maturity into the designs. She didn't want to listen to what they said because she believed she was at her best now and needed to be 'discovered'. She continued with her aggressive behavior, demanding more work, criticizing and belittling her coworkers, and even using bribes to acquire information about future projects.

She was climbing the corporate ladder now in a very unscrupulous way. This beautiful, young, talented girl whom everyone loved because she was so very kind and generous was developing into a very nasty person who was intent on removing anyone on her path to success.

She closed her mind to any hurt that she inflicted on coworkers and even friends if they made comments about her behavior. Many of her friends just distanced themselves from her. The new designers assigned to work under her guidance were constantly degraded for their work. She brought many of them to tears with her criticisms.

We angels watched very closely now as this young girl continued to choose the wrong paths to follow in life. She was headed for disaster if she continued this way and would not complete her life plan that she had written here in heaven.

She was given her artistic talent to help others. Her main goal on earth was to guide and help those less fortunate to rise up and succeed in life. She was on earth to help and influence others to stand on their feet and learn to take care of themselves so that they could turn around and extend their hands to help others. It was a circle that she drew on her life plan...*I have the talent to reach out to help you, then you reach out to help another who reaches out to help and the chain of helping hands grows longer and stronger.* As a spirit, she was very proud of her plan to reach out and help thousands of souls on earth.

She developed her talent very well but did not open her heart to help others. She was stuck in her own circle to be successful and to be recognized by the world as a great fashion designer. She wanted fame and fortune. She viewed her monetary income as true success.

She was becoming totally earthbound and tied to the trappings of greed, selfishness and power. We angels were very alarmed that the young girl had moved far away from her written plan. If she continued with this life style, she would not fulfill what she had written and would have to return to earth to try again. We needed to act quickly and strongly to help her change her destructive way of life.

Her reputation as a nasty but talented fashion designer was now well known throughout the industry. She was oblivious to the negative articles and reviews written in many magazines and newspapers. She liked to see her name in print no matter what was written, be it good or bad.

She was commissioned by her company to design a wedding dress and wardrobe for a very high dignitary in a foreign country. She was ecstatic to receive the honor to show her designs at this high level. She worked day and night with the designers that she chose to help her with this enormous job. Her staff worked feverishly to keep up with her demands. She was brutal to them, repeatedly tearing up their work, ripping apart intricate details sewed on expensive fabric. Several workers just walked away saying that their name next to her name would destroy their own career.

One afternoon, the foreign dignitary, who commissioned the work, walked into the studio unannounced. He was appalled at what he saw and heard. The young designer was shaking her finger in the face of a worker, shouting and degrading her. The young worker was fearful and in tears. The dignitary walked quickly to the young designer and put his hand between the workers face and the finger that was almost touching the worker's face. The young designer did not look at whose hand had just appeared and promptly pushed it away.

He then bellowed, **YOU'RE FIRED**!

She turned quickly to face him and quickly changed her demeanor. In a very quiet and sweet voice she welcomed him to her studio and asked if he would like to view some of the completed fashions that he had requested. He just stared at her hardly believing the change in personality. She turned on the 'charm' he experienced the first time that he met her.

He asked, 'do you always treat your workers like they are slaves'?

She stated that she did not understand what he was saying. She said that the worker needed to be reprimanded for some costly errors.

He told her that no one should ever be talked to or treated in the manner he had just witnessed. He said that he could see fear in all the workers in the room and 'it is YOU that they fear'.

'These people are good people', he said. 'They are not animals that you can just push around. You may be a good designer and you may think that you are better than you really are, but you are not'.

'Let this be a lesson to you...*no matter how hard you work and how skilled you are in your field, there is always someone a lot better than you'.*

'In your case, there are many. Before I leave, I will pay your staff for the mental pain and suffering they endured trying to help YOU succeed. I ask that they all leave with me'.

The young designer watched as her studio emptied. It was eerily quiet. She had no tears in her eyes nor any remorse in her heart. She just stood and stared at the door. She gently turned around and stared at the beautiful dresses she had designed. Her envisioned prestigious audiences would never admire them. A tear finally formed in her eyes. How can this be, she thought? I am a great designer. Now the tears finally flowed from her eyes.

Upon returning to the office the following week, she was notified that she was no longer needed. She walked out of the building in total disbelief. Again, not understanding how she could be fired when she was the best designer in the company.

She sat on a bench in a nearby park. She sat and just stared, thinking of nothing. An elderly gentleman quietly sat beside her. She paid no attention to him. He quietly said 'good morning' to which she did not respond.

'Have you ever thought of using your artistic talents to help others', he asked?

She quickly turned to him and asked harshly how he knew her background? He responded that he had seen her at many fashion shows and that he knew her designs. He told her that she was quite talented but that he also knew of several other designers that showed a lot more talent and maturity in their work.

'Well', she responded, 'I wasn't fired for lack of maturity'.

'I was let go for disciplining my employees'. She continued, 'I believe employees need to be kept in line and follow my orders'.

He shook his head and softly told her that she was going about it in the wrong way.

'You believed you were great and above everyone who worked for you. In fact, you believed that you were better and more talented that your coworkers. Listen to me carefully. *No one is any better than anyone else.* You have totally moved away from the caring and loving person that you were as a child and even when you were a young adult'.

'What happened to you'?

'When did you become so selfish, blind and egotistical'?

'You have no love in your heart'.

'Do you think this spells success? Think about this and think very hard'.

'This is your life, live it fully and with love'.

When she looked up to answer him, the bench was empty. She looked up and down the street but saw no one.

Within the next year, the young designer could be found in neighborhood gathering centers teaching and guiding the old and the young in many aspects of art. She was truly loved by everyone she worked with at these centers.

What happened?

Yes, this was a true miracle...one that occurs frequently without any fanfare or television or newspaper reports.

We angels watched very closely as the young designer moved further and further away from her life plan. We directed the dignitary who commissioned her designs to visit her work studio unannounced.

When she was let go at her place of employment, we saw that she still had no remorse for her actions. She had no idea of how badly she treated her employees and how she hurt them mentally.

The elderly gentleman who sat next to her on the park bench was indeed one of us. We saw that she really needed our help, our understanding and some strong words of advice. When our angel left, we watched closely hoping that she would receive his words and change her selfish life to a life filled with love.

When you hear stories, and there are many, of someone suddenly making a positive turn from a selfish or destructive lifestyle, know that this is as strong a miracle as a 'near death experience'.

Miracles are occurring every day; people on earth just pay attention to the high profile, death-defying ones.

Look around you now.

Count how many miracles you see or hear or read about in one week.

Recognize the small, silent miracles that are occurring around you and around the world.

Now look at your life. Have you experienced a miracle in your lifetime?

-Archangel Anrielle

As I mentioned above, 'silent miracles' are occurring every day throughout the world. These miracles occur at all levels of society, as well as on all levels of government. When you read about an aggressive government wanting and trying to take over its neighboring countries and suddenly slowing or stopping its aggressive actions, you might say that something/someone within the government caused this action. Many at higher government levels look for interventions that might be occurring behind closed doors.

All of that is possible, but always look for interventions coming from our side. We angels are always on alert to intervene at all government levels to avert major destruction on earth. When necessary, angels will assume human form and maneuver meetings to bring major disputes to discussion tables. We work to guide destructive military forces into situations that will either slow or stop their harmful actions. We are always present with the many military forces who are trying to stop aggressive nations. They are successful when they follow our signs and messages.

When you see or read about sudden changes in world events, you may wonder why something stopped or slowed. Look for us angels. We are the force behind every great change that occurs to bring peace on earth.

A 'silent miracle' can happen to your next-door neighbor, a family member, a friend or even the person on the street corner asking you for pennies as you pass by. When you see a sudden or even gradual turnaround in a person's behavior, know that we angels worked to help that person readjust their destructive lifestyle.

These small miracles include destructive health habits that could cause a person to become debilitated and not be physically able to complete their written life plan before returning to us.

The same is true for destructive behavior that would cause a person to injure another person or even himself.

Another example of 'silent miracles' is seen with those who become complacent in life. They have no ambition and just float through life on a day-to-day basis. They are not aware of what is happening around them and exhibit no love for themselves or others. They are just spending time on earth with no intent of advancing their souls.

We are very aware of these personalities and the help that they need before they drift too far away from their written plan. We work feverishly to direct and guide them. When a soul turns around and seems to 'wake up' to his true existence on earth, there is much jubilation here in heaven.

As you witness these small changes, know you are witnessing true miracles.

-Archangel Anrielle

Several young boys in the neighborhood always gathered once a week at a local gym to play basketball. They were young teens and all came from hard-working families. Sometimes, several of the parents accompanied the boys to the gym to cheer them on.

The boys were exposed to all the temptations that life offers young teens. Their parents worked very hard to instill sound and moral judgment in their sons. They were all proud of their children. As time passed and the boys separated, attending different high schools, they promised to reconnect every month to check on each other's progress. They did this for about two years and slowly they grew apart due to other interests and the demands of their schools.

Before graduating from high school, the boys reached out to each other for a reunion. Several got together but three were missing. The boys who came together were saddened that not everyone could attend.

We angels were closely watching the three boys who did not join their friends before graduation. One young boy had already dropped out of high school. He was an 'A' student but slowly slipped to a failing level, receiving warnings from his teachers. He kept this information from his parents who thought he was going to school every day as he left early in the morning.

The other two boys remained in school but spent their free time with their friend who dropped out of school. We angels could see they were all starting to aimlessly wander away from their life plans. We worked to direct them back onto their paths especially the young boy who had dropped out of school.

We presented them with opportunities to attend professional sports events at their school. We tried to direct their attention to the advertisements concerning alcohol and driving, and how to help others less fortunate than themselves. Our intent was to show them that they had everything at their fingertips to succeed in life. They needed to apply themselves in school and with their families to cement the groundwork for success not only materialistically but also spiritually. They also needed to incorporate the groundwork that their parents and families had provided when they were little children.

We followed all three boys as they continued down this path. After high school, they stayed connected with each other and none of them pursued any advanced education. Their parents were devastated but knew they couldn't force their sons to lead successful lives as each parent envisioned. They all just watched their sons walk away to a new life where the boys believed they would be free to express themselves.

As expected the boys went downhill from there. They traveled and slept and ate and did nothing with their lives except to say they were 'experiencing' life. Alcohol became a major staple in their lives at this time and they drank freely. They figured out a panhandling gig that brought them enough money to exist at this level.

The boys were totally ignoring our signs and messages. Their eyes needed to be opened for them to really see themselves and the waste they were becoming.

As they were driving drunk one evening, the driver fell asleep and veered off the road. The car crashed into a tree. The area was mountainous and deserted. The temperature was dropping quickly. Two of the boys lay unconscious in the front seat. The young boy who was very intelligent and had dropped out of high school lay stunned in the back seat. He quickly sobered up and jumped out of the car. Looking around, he realized they were in for a long night with no other cars in sight.

He started shivering. He checked his two friends in the front seat and saw they were breathing but he didn't know the extent of their injuries. He tried to start the car in order to get heat for himself and his friends but the engine was damaged and would not start.

He remembered they all had their suitcases in the trunk. He tried to open the trunk but that too was damaged. He was becoming frightened now and started to panic. He was always in control of his life and environment and now the environment was taking over. He did not like this feeling. He paced, thinking and trying to keep warm.

We sent him messages to return to the car. We directed his eyes to the back seat to show him that the seats folded down to give access to the trunk. This was his 'aha' moment receiving our message to pull the back seat down and get the suitcases. He now frantically scrambled in the dark of night to open the suitcases to find warm clothes. He covered his friends with all of their clothes and returned to the back seat to cover himself.

The wind was strong in the mountains that night. The young boy was extremely scared with the wind howling and the rustling of the bushes from animals passing nearby. We continued to send him messages of comfort and love. He finally screamed out to us and to God asking us where we were. He wanted to know how God could let this happen to him. He said that he believed that he was a good person even though he hadn't done anything constructive with his life. He said to us that he just wanted to have 'fun' in life.

Several hours had passed since the accident. It was extremely cold and windy.

The young man in the back seat had convinced himself that they were all going to die before the sun came up.

His two friends in the front seat started to stir. The young man jumped into action, relieved they were regaining consciousness. He immediately talked to them to see if they hurt anywhere. They both answered they had no pain but they were cold. He told them to stay under all the clothes he piled on them encouraging them to be positive in order to stay alive. Don't think cold, he said, think hot. They laughed at him. But, somehow, they knew he was serious.

'Keep talking', he urged them, 'stay awake. Let's sing some songs'.

'WE MUST STAY AWAKE' he hollered at them.

As the sun came upon the horizon, the exhausted boys spotted a truck's headlights coming their way. They all jumped out of the car waving their hands for help. The truck slowed when the driver saw the car had smashed into a tree. He told the three young men to climb into the truck. He told them that there was no phone signal in the area so he was not able to call for help.

The truck driver drove them directly to a nearby hospital. The boys were treated for hypothermia and released the following day. One of the doctors remarked to the young man who covered his friends with their clothes from the suitcases and made them stay awake during the cold night that he had saved his friends lives. All of you would have died from exposure and hypothermia if not for the calm thinking and actions of your friend. The doctor continued to say that the young man had the potential to be a good leader in whatever profession he chose.

The three young men returned to their hometown and reunited with their families. They related their harrowing experience in the mountains and all stated to their families that they were now prepared to walk through life. They realized that they needed more skills and a different perspective on life in order to survive.

They then met with their high school buddies to relate this experience and to tell them they were ready to 'grow up'. One of their friends smiled and quietly told them that they had just experienced a 'miracle'. He said that he hopes they recognized their miracle. He continued saying that they were protected on the mountain because they have important tasks to complete in life before they return to the other side.

'You know', he said, 'the truck driver was probably an angel that came along to rescue all three of you'.

The three young boys looked at each other and then at their friend with tears in their eyes and said 'thank you' in unison.

We angels were ecstatic to have influenced the movement of these three boys back onto their life plans before they drifted too far off course.

As you can see, these small 'silent miracles' may take time, maybe one month, one year or even many years.

The main goal is to always get a soul back onto its life plan before that soul transitions back to heaven.

Are you presently walking on your designated path towards God?

-Archangel Anrielle

CONCLUSION

When you hear of a great 'miracle' that has just occurred and you shout 'thank God', we angels want you to take another minute to look for us in that 'miracle' story.

Think about it.

Where can you see us in the story?

Did a stranger walk in to give the survivor some advice or push them out of harm's way?

Know that stranger was one of us; the stranger was an angel.

When a cancer patient 'miraculously' moves into complete recovery, can you see us helping? That patient had more work to do on earth so we guided the medical staff with the selection of the patient's therapy process. The patient will tell you about the doctor's great medical skills but look past that. Know that it was us angels who directed the doctor in choosing the appropriate chemotherapy regimen.

Alcohol and drug abuse/addiction are rampant on earth right now. We angels are very busy pulling many souls out of the gripping bonds of abuse and addiction. We are working continuously with those souls so that they may become strong enough to seek help and move into the recovery phase. The souls who are experiencing addiction must move out of their addicted state to complete their true purpose on earth.

We are also working with researchers and medical personnel to guide them to develop new drugs and methods to help addicted souls and cancer patients.

So, look for us when you see a friend or relative or even a stranger suffering from addiction. Know that we are working to direct them to medical shelters capable of addressing their specific addicted needs.

Also, when an addicted soul receives lifesaving help from a policeman or fireman or medical professional, know we were present and guided their actions.

You can see us angels and our 'miracles' every day. You just need to raise your awareness.

Look at your own life now. Surely, you have had difficult and maybe even scary events in your life.

Do you wonder how you survived?

Think of all the circumstances surrounding your events and see where we played a part to help you get back to living your written life plan.

We were there, I guarantee, but you did not recognize us.

We are with you now as we were back then.

So, call on us, talk to us and ask us to direct you to the best path possible to move you closer to God.

Always know that we love you. We are your ambassadors to God.

-Archangel Sebastian

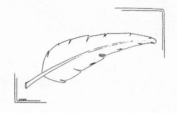

YOUR PERSONAL MIRACLES